MR. CLAUDE

MR. CLAUDE

By
Ada Morehead Holland

Texas A&M University Press
COLLEGE STATION

Library of Congress Cataloging in Publication Data

Holland, Ada Morehead.
    Mr. Claude.

    Bibliography: p.
    1. Kennedy, Claude Barr, 1869–1963.   2. Houston Coun-
ty (Tex.)—Biography.   3. Trinity County (Tex.)—Biography.
4. Sawmills—Texas—Trinity County—History.   5. Sawmills
—Texas—Houston County—History.   6. Houston County
(Tex.)—Social life and customs.   7. Trinity County (Tex.)—So-
cial life and customs.   I. Title.
F392.H7K464   1984   976.4′17206′0924   83-40502
ISBN 0-89096-182-4

Manufactured in the United States of America
FIRST EDITION

In Memory of Wilbur

Contents

List of Illustrations

MAP

Preface

I set out to write a book about life in that almost mythical place we refer to as "the piney woods of deep East Texas." I wanted it to reflect the lumber industry, because for the past one hundred years that industry has dominated the area. I searched for an interesting character to carry the story. When I met Fred Kennedy and heard him speak of his father I knew I had found my man.

Claude Barr Kennedy lived and worked and reared his family at the time big sawmills dotted East Texas and consumed the virgin pine forests. His story is the story of life in the sawmill towns. But it is more than that. It is the story of East Texas itself.

"Mr. Claude" descended from a pioneer grandfather who migrated to Texas from Mississippi in the early days of the Republic of Texas, when a man had literally to carve out of the forest a life for himself and his wife and children. His ancestors survived the privations of the early days, plus the upheaval of the Civil War and the impoverishment of its aftermath, and handed down by word of mouth, from generation to generation, the family's history, its joys and its sorrows. And Mr. Claude, in his turn, passed on what had been told to him, plus interesting stories from his own life.

I found written records here and there: references to old deeds in a few books that survived the several fires at the Houston County courthouse, census reports for the Republic of Texas and for the United States, Civil War records in the National Archives, data compiled by an oil company when it wanted to lease a piece of property, old newspaper clippings, some memoirs, various histories of Texas and of East Texas counties.

But I gathered the tales and most of what makes this book from interviews with Mr. Claude's children and grandchildren.

Acknowledgements

In my search for information I had gracious assistance from many people. I wish especially to acknowledge the help of Clyde Thompson, vice-president, and Linda Dorsett, assistant director of public affairs, at Temple-Eastex, Incorporated, Diboll, Texas; E. R. Waggoner, executive vice-president of Texas Forest Association and curator of Texas Forestry Museum, Lufkin, Texas; Gilbert Woodman, retired engineer, Alhambra, California; William Schworer, Balboa Island, California; Lloyd J. Gregory, M.D., Houston, Texas; Willie Earl Tindall and Pamela Lynn Palmer, librarians at Stephen F. Austin University, Nacogdoches, Texas; Sallie Woodward and her staff at Crockett Public Library, A. B. Brown, M.D., Russell Paul of Paul's Coins, Tokens and Jewelry, Lee E. Wells, Kate McLendon, Frank and Viola Allen, Chester Rosson, John C. Smith, Don Currey, Eugene Harrison, and Eliza Bishop, all of Crockett, Texas; Ava Bush, Grapeland, Texas; Wyncie Dell Barnhill, Old Randolph, Texas; Mack Steed, Kennard, Texas; and, of course, members of the Kennedy family.

I am indebted to my friends Frank and Rosemary Wardlaw, Lulu Brand, Ruth Pennybacker, and Shirley Bridgwater for encouragement and for critical reading of the manuscript.

Also, I wish to acknowledge my large debt to my loving and supportive family for their enthusiasm and confidence, and for numerous critical readings of the manuscript.

GENEALOGY: THE KENNEDY FAMILY

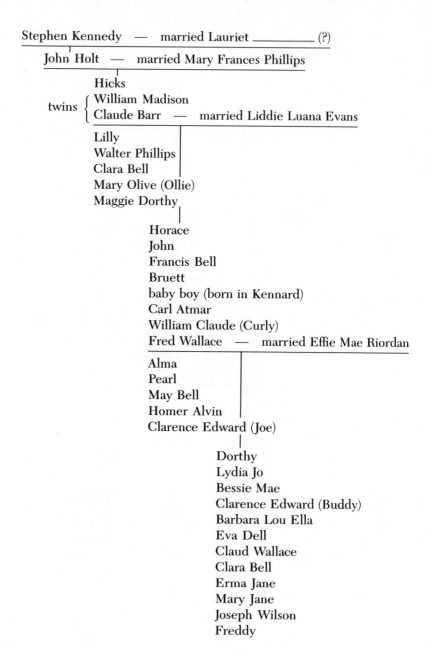

Stephen Kennedy — married Lauriet _____ (?)

John Holt — married Mary Frances Phillips

Hicks

twins { William Madison

Claude Barr — married Liddie Luana Evans

Lilly
Walter Phillips
Clara Bell
Mary Olive (Ollie)
Maggie Dorthy

Horace
John
Francis Bell
Bruett
baby boy (born in Kennard)
Carl Atmar
William Claude (Curly)
Fred Wallace — married Effie Mae Riordan

Alma
Pearl
May Bell
Homer Alvin
Clarence Edward (Joe)

Dorthy
Lydia Jo
Bessie Mae
Clarence Edward (Buddy)
Barbara Lou Ella
Eva Dell
Claud Wallace
Clara Bell
Erma Jane
Mary Jane
Joseph Wilson
Freddy

PART I

These chapters were pieced together by the author. They are based on material gathered from interviews with members of the Kennedy family—material substantiated and supplemented by information obtained through research.

Chapter 1

Mr. Claude always said his earliest memory was of the day his father, John Holt Kennedy, cut the end off a hoe handle, put the stub-handled hoe in his son's hands and took him to the field and showed him how to chop cotton. That was in the spring of 1874, nine years after the end of the Civil War. The boy Claude was four years old.

It was then, while his father John Holt and his mother Mary chopped cotton and hoed corn—and while his baby sister Lilly and his semi-invalid, six-year-old brother Hicks played on a pallet in the shade of a big oak at the edge of the field—that young Claude began to earn his keep. He learned to stay close to patient, easygoing John Holt, because Mary often was out of sorts and might swat him if she saw him make a mistake and cut off a big healthy cotton plant or cover up a hill of corn.

Sometimes in the evening after supper, while Mary washed the dishes and did whatever had to be done for baby Lilly, John Holt took his two sons on his lap and told them of their grand-father Stephen Kennedy who had trekked in the early 1800s from Mississippi to Louisiana and then over a trail called the Old San Antonio Road until he came here to San Pedro Creek, deep in the piney woods of East Texas, where he settled down. He told how Stephen and his wife Lauriet and a few other families cleared small pieces of land, built log-cabin homes, drove off the Indians, and made themselves a community where they could raise their food and their families, a community which by John

Holt's time was flanked by a little pioneer town called Augusta, in the northern part of Houston County.

He bragged about how Stephen had received a grant of one league and a labor of land (more than 4,500 acres) from the government of the Republic of Texas after it won its independence from Mexico. The fact that Stephen had not bothered to secure a legal title to that land, and so had not held onto it, was not stressed. It had been wild uncleared land, out in the middle of the forest, at a time when that kind of land was often considered more of a liability than an asset. What a man needed then was a small tract of cleared land on which he could raise enough vegetables to feed his family, enough corn to feed a cow and a couple of oxen—horses if he was fortunate enough to have any—plus a few ears with which to coax his hogs out of the woods at butchering time, and a bale or two of cotton to take to the new county seat of Crockett and trade for necessities he could not raise on the farm. East Texas was covered then with big trees, mostly pines and oaks, and these had to be cut and burned before the sun could get to the fields to make the crops grow. Except for the few that were needed for building cabins and barns and for heating and cooking, trees were a nuisance.

John Holt talked about what he called log rollings, when a new family moved into the area, or a couple got married, and the whole neighborhood gathered to help clear a field. Generally, the owner would have chopped down the trees already and removed the tops and limbs, and cut the trunks into logs that would be scattered over the field, too heavy for one man to move. Each neighbor would bring with him his hand spike, a strong pole, usually of dogwood. Several of these poles would be slipped under a log, sticking out far enough so that a man on each side could get a handhold. With three or four hand spikes and twice as many men, the logs could be carried to a place in the center of the field and rolled onto a pile to be burned. When the men arrived with a log, those along one side would prop their ends of the hand spikes against the logs already there and the men along the other side would raise their ends and roll the log onto the pile. The logs were piled in long rows called windrows. On the first day there was a good wind the farmer would set fire to the windward end and hope the wind would carry the fire all the way up the row and burn up all the logs. Then he could plant his field.

John Holt said people liked log rollings. Whole families gathered for these occasions. While the men piled the logs into windrows the women cooked and the children played. If the log rolling was held at an already established home, there was generally a quilt in the frame, and some of the women quilted while others dressed chickens and made dumplings that they cooked in an iron washpot in the yard. They made coffee in big pots in the yard, too. There was always corn pone, baked in Dutch ovens. Once in a while there were flour biscuits, and sometimes even Dutch-oven pies made of wild plums or wild blackberries, sweetened with syrup made from homegrown cane. Everybody enjoyed log rollings.

A time would come, after he was a man, when Claude would remember these tales of wasted timber and unclaimed land, and wonder about it, and wish it could have been different.

John Holt said hardly any of the first settlers bought land. Stephen and the others simply picked out a place that looked good, cleared it, and built a cabin. Later, most of them did get titles to their land, but they had been living on it for a number of years before they did. John Holt had inherited his land, uncleared, from his mother, who had received it as a gift from one of her relatives when John Holt was a boy. He told his sons how he had cleared it, chopping down the trees with a double-bitted ax and inviting the neighbors in for a log rolling, how he and Mary had then built their house of rough boards he'd had sawed at a little wood-burning, steam-powered sawmill near by. He said it was called a lumber house, and Claude could tell his father was proud to have that kind of house.

Sometimes Mary would get tired of all this talk while she worked. She'd say, "Put them younguns down and go get a bucket of water, and bring in some stovewood. Looks like I'm the only one can see anything to do around this shack."

But Claude knew his mother didn't really consider their home a shack—he knew she was proud of it. She'd tell him, "Clean that mud off your feet before you come in this house! A body'd think you was used to living in a log cabin with a dirt floor!" He noticed that she not only often worked into the night straightening the house and scrubbing the floor with ashes and a mop made of corn shucks, but that she pulled every weed and every blade of grass she caught growing in their yard, and kept the yard swept clean with a broom made of dogwood brush. He knew, too, that she was proud of her cast-iron cookstove that saved her a lot of the stooping and squatting that women who still cooked in fireplaces had to do. (The stove had been a wedding gift. Mary had inveigled her father—Old Madison Phillips, who owned hundreds of acres of land in Anderson County that he had worked with slaves, and who was tight-fisted as all get out—into giving it to her.)

When John Holt and Mary married shortly after he came home from the Civil War they cleared their land and built their lumber house and started out full of hope. John Holt had spent four years fighting for the Confederacy and had come home with a wounded leg that still hurt. But he *had* come home, and he *did* own land. Also, the area around San Pedro Creek had escaped the devastation the war had inflicted on most of the South—it was pretty much as he had left it when he enlisted.

His homecoming was marred by the fact that his father Stephen had lost his life in the war and his mother Lauriet also had died before John Holt got home. But the land was there, and John Holt and Mary believed they could make it produce for them. Their parents had taught them the three Rs (there were no public schools there when they were growing up) and the merits of hard work. They felt prepared for life. That was in 1865.

Now, in 1873, their outlook was not as bright. Of the five children who had been born to them, only three were alive. And of these, only Claude and Lilly were healthy. Their firstborn, Hicks, a sickly child, was said to have rheumatism, and Claude's twin, William Madison, and a little boy named Walter Phillips, who was two years younger than Lilly, had both died in infancy.

For eight years they had struggled along, trying to hold themselves and their little family together. They had gone deeper and deeper in debt at the general store, each year planting a crop that could not be sold for money—because there *was* no money, only barter—each year failing to produce enough on their land to pay for what they had bought at the store.

Like her husband, Mary remembered a childhood when there was plenty to eat and wear, when life was easier. But, unlike her husband, she seldom spoke of it.

One day John Holt came in from the field and found Mary whipping Claude. He stood there until she got through, and Claude had gone off under the house to commiserate with himself, and then he said, "You whipped him pretty hard."

She said, "Well, sometimes he makes me so mad I jest want to tear him up."

John Holt said, "What did he do?"

She said, "I sent him to put the chickens up, and he killed one of my best hens with a rock, jest because he was having trouble getting her to go in the pen!"

John Holt said, "Well, now we can have chicken and dumplings."

Mary stomped over and picked up the dead hen.

After supper that night John Holt held Claude on his lap for a long time, and told him how things used to be.

Perhaps reminiscing gave John Holt relief from the harsh life he and Mary and their children were now reduced to. At any rate, many an evening found him holding his little son and filling him with his own nostalgia, with his memories of a happy, productive childhood, when hard work could be depended upon to reward a person with all the necessities and even a few luxuries.

He told of the prosperous times after Texas joined the United States, and before the Civil War broke out, when the government set up post offices and started rural mail delivery. "You could write a letter to somebody in Mississippi or Louisiana and just put it in your mailbox down by the road, and the mail carrier would come by on his horse and pick it up and send it on. You didn't have to take letters all the way to Augusta in them days. And sometimes wasn't more'n a month till you found an answer to that letter, right there in your box. Seemed like letters hardly ever got lost like they do now.

[7]

"And we could sell anything we raised that we didn't need, like corn or potatoes or bacon, stuff like that. You could even sell things for real money. You didn't have to take it out in trade."

Times *had* been better. Even before Texas joined the United States, while it was still a struggling young republic, times had been better. Stephen Kennedy had been prominent in the little community on San Pedro Creek and in newly formed Houston County, being twice elected to the office of justice of the peace. And when the county needed to levy taxes for a new courthouse or something Stephen's name appeared on the petition that was sent to the governor in Austin. Lauriet had inherited 500 acres of good land on San Pedro Creek, that Stephen had not even cleared because what he had taken up when he first settled there was more than enough for one family to work. Perhaps that is why Stephen didn't go to the trouble to prove up title to and clear his large grant of land back in the forest.

John Holt told how a man came around taking the census. He said, "Mama got insulted because the man said we didn't have nothing in the house that was worth anything except our clock. One metal clock, that's all he wrote down. And there was our table, and chairs, and the big bed—all them things Papa had made, and Mama was so proud of."

He told about the house, that was two log cabins built about ten feet apart and connected by a roof over the whole thing. "The roof was made out of rived boards, just like ours is. But the chimley wasn't made out of bricks. It was a cat-and-stick chimley, like them you see in some of these old log houses around here. Everybody had that kind then. It had a frame of little poles that was covered with handfuls of mud mixed with Spanish moss. Some people mixed their cats with straw, but ours was mixed with moss."

He said Stephen had made puncheon floors in both their cabins. "He split the logs and hewed down the split side and laid them with that side up. It was a good floor, almost as smooth as this here board floor we've got."

It was true that during the 1850s, when John Holt was a boy, times in East Texas were good. The small towns of Crockett

[8]

and Augusta served thriving communities. There were two hotels and two general merchandise stores in Crockett, and one of each in Augusta. Crockett had a drugstore, a few practicing physicians, and a visiting dentist, plus numerous small shops and a weekly newspaper. Country doctors rode horseback and carried surgical instruments and medicine in saddlebags. Blacksmith and wagon shops did a good business in both Crockett and Augusta, cabinet shops made furniture, buildings were erected of brick made in the community.

By the time the boy Claude was born in 1869 East Texas had been prostrated by a war few people wanted, fought over slaves few Texans possessed. It had smarted through years of corrupt reconstruction governors and carpetbagger-controlled elected officials. Stephen Kennedy had enlisted in the war and had died while serving with the Confederate forces in New Mexico. John Holt had enlisted in that war, too, and had fought as part of Company A, First Regiment, Texas Volunteers, in many of the important battles—Malvern Hill, the Wilderness, Gettysburg and the rest—right up to the end of the war. He had been cited for bravery and commissioned in the field, had been wounded and had walked with a limp ever since. But Claude never found out much about that from his father. John Holt didn't like to talk about it. He did tell his son, "General Grant turned me loose on May 15, 1865. Me and the other Confederate soldiers. We'd been prisoners ever since the Confederates decided to give up. They called it *paroling* us when they turned us loose and said we could come home. May 15, 1865. I'll never forget that day."

Following the war there was lawlessness, when each man had to protect himself and family any way he could. And there were hard times, when nearly every man, woman, and child knew drudgery and hunger. Money was almost nonexistent. What a farmer and his family could raise, or barter for, was all they had. And people in town fared little better. In 1868 the Crockett *Sentinel* ran an advertisement: "To meet the stringency of the times . . . we will in future receive corn, pork, potatoes, eggs, chickens, or butter for subscriptions."

The fledgling communities in East Texas had been knocked

down by the war and kicked by its aftermath, and life would be hard for most of their people for years to come. Perhaps it was good that the little boy sitting on John Holt's lap, looking with him into a happy past, could not see into the future.

Chapter 2

A part of his life that Mr. Claude remembered well, and one he liked to tell his children and grandchildren about, was when his father was a deputy sheriff.

He said that one day when he and the other children were in Augusta with their parents they saw the sheriff and a couple of his deputies riding around town on beautiful horses, with big shiny revolvers hanging at their sides. After that Claude and Lilly—Hicks, too, when he wasn't too sick—played sheriff-and-robbers, galloping around on pole horses, firing away with stick revolvers. So of course they were delighted when John Holt came home one day and announced, "The sheriff wants me to be a deputy."

Mr. Claude said, "I threw my cap in the air and jumped up and down. Lilly run to Papa and started dancing around him. Papa said, 'Whoa! I ain't governor of Texas yet.'"

But Mary didn't like the idea. She looked at John Holt for a long time and said, "You ain't fixing to do it, are you?"

He leaned against the doorcasing, took his thumb and pushed his hat back from his forehead, and said, "I was kinda figuring on it."

That night Claude heard John Holt and Mary arguing. She said, "Who's gonna work the farm? I can't—I'm always with a youngun in my arms and another'n in my belly."

John Holt said, "Aw, Mary, it's not gonna take me away from home much. Being a deputy don't take a lot of a feller's time. I can still farm. And another thing," he told her, "they'll pay me in real money. Where else we gonna get any money?"

Mary said, "Well, we could use some money."

After a while John Holt said, "I'll have to get a saddle horse."

"And jest what you gonna pay for a horse with?" Mary wanted to know.

"Old man Davis said he'd let me have a horse and whatever I need," he told her.

Mary said, "That don't sound like Davis. The last time I's in the store he was dunning me for some corn—said he wasn't gonna carry us much longer without we paid him something."

John Holt said, "I guess he thinks if I get to earning money being a deputy we can start paying something on our bill."

"Well," said Mary, "I guess you're dead set on doing it. I guess there ain't nothing more to say."

"I'll have to go to Augusta tomorrow and get the horse and things," he told her. "And we'll have to sign a bond."

Claude didn't hear Mary say anything more. He didn't realize then that this was a conversation that would become important to him, that he would wonder about years later, and try to recall exactly.

The next morning John Holt hitched the two workhorses to the wagon and they all climbed in and went to Augusta. Mary and John Holt signed the paper he had told her about. She didn't try to read it—she probably wouldn't have understood it if she had, written as it was in the language of lawyers.

Mary and the children went home in the wagon. John Holt rode proudly beside them, on his new horse, sitting in his new saddle, with his new revolver at his side.

But it wasn't long before John Holt realized that being a deputy sheriff was more time consuming than he had expected. Richard Bennett Hubbard, who became governor in 1876, was determined to bring law and order to Texas, and to lift the state out of the chaos in which it had been floundering since the end of the war. He offered rewards for the capture of criminals and put pressure on local officials to bring outlaws in for trial.

John Holt began saddling his horse in the morning and keeping it saddled all day, because he never knew when somebody would come riding up with a message from the sheriff. He often had to ride off in the middle of the day, leaving Claude and Lilly to work alone in the field. Lilly hated the work and usually fought with Claude over who would do what. Sometimes Mary could hear them, all the way to the house, and would have to come out and stop the argument. She generally settled it by whipping both of them. But the next day they'd be at it again. One day Claude took his hoe handle to Lilly. Finally Mary started leaving Lilly at the house to care for the younger children (they had two more little girls by now—Clara Bell who was three and Mary Olive who was still a baby), and Mary herself worked in the field.

One afternoon a boy came rushing up on a horse that was white with lather, right into the field where John Holt and Mary and Claude were working. He said the sheriff needed John Holt in a hurry, that there was a murderer holed up in a house at Stubblefield, in the southern part of the county, threatening to shoot anybody who came near. The sheriff wanted John Holt to go down there and bring the man in.

John Holt laid down his hoe and started for his already saddled horse. Mary turned in anger to the boy who had brought the message. "Why don't the sheriff go get that man hisself? It ain't the place of no deputy to do what the sheriff is too scared to do!"

John Holt climbed into the saddle and said, "Now . . . Mary."

"You're gonna get yourself killed, that's what you're gonna do!" she called after him as he and the boy galloped off. She turned around to find Claude standing there, terrified. "Well, get to work!" she screamed at him. "What are you standing there gawking about?"

Around midnight John Holt rode in, whistling Dixie. He had talked the man into surrendering. No shots had been fired.

When Claude was eight years old John Holt decided it was time to teach his sons to read and write and figure a little. The only books they had were the Bible that had belonged to his parents and an old McGuffey's Reader that Stephen had used when he taught John Holt to read and write. John Holt got these out of

[13]

the trunk, and after the evening meal, while Mary washed the dishes and tidied the kitchen, he sat Claude and Hicks at the kitchen table and attempted to educate them.

Sometimes, when they were at the house waiting for Mary to get the noon meal on the table, John Holt would draw numbers in the sand of the clean-swept yard and show his sons how to add or subtract. And once Mary caught John Holt and Claude on their knees, between the corn rows, working division problems in a place they had smoothed out in the soft dirt of the cornfield.

One day John Holt rode in from Augusta with two new slates and two slate pencils. Mary said, "Why'd you buy two of them things? One would been a plenty." But the boys were delighted and excited and they and John Holt started right in writing and working problems on the fine new slates. Nobody paid any attention to Mary's lack of enthusiasm.

Mr. Claude said it was when he was about nine years old that the man named Davis took possession of their farm. The document John Holt and Mary had signed when he became a deputy sheriff turned out to be a warranty deed, giving Davis the right to take their farm in case they did not pay what they owed him.

Mary believed Davis had deceived her, and she remained angry about it for the rest of her life. Claude was never sure whether she also believed John Holt had deceived her. And Claude, himself, was never sure about that, either. He often tried to reconstruct the conversation he had overheard that night before they signed the document, but he was never able to decide whether his father knew what they were being asked to sign.

Mr. Claude said Davis took the farm and gave them an old hotel in Augusta, and wrote off what they owed at the store. By this time a new town called Grapeland was growing up along the new railroad a few miles away, and Augusta was already beginning to die. The hotel was of little value. But now it was the only home they had.

Mary ran the hotel, cleaning the rooms and cooking for the few guests who now and then stayed there. John Holt continued to work as a deputy sheriff.

There was a public school in Augusta then, and young Claude was enrolled. Children from the age of eight to sixteen were entitled to go. School was held four months each year.

Mr. Claude remembered only a few things about living at the hotel. One was that there was a killing there while they were operating the hotel. A couple of guests were scuffling over a gun, and one man shot the other.

And one thing he remembered vividly was that one night John Holt was asked to go out and track down some horse thieves. A cold rain was turning to sleet. John Holt had a bad cold, and Mary tried to talk him into waiting until morning, but he felt it was his duty to go while the trail was fresh. Mary became very angry, but he went and was gone all night. When he came home there was ice in his beard, ice in the folds of his clothes.

In less than a week John Holt was dead of pneumonia.

Mr. Claude said he and the other children thought Mary might lose her mind after their father died. He said, "Her temper had always been fiery, but seemed like it got worse. She'd whip us, unreasonable, for nothing, hardly. One time she whipped me till big knots swelled up on my legs because I ate some cooked butterbeans she was saving for supper. I didn't know that's all we had for supper. I was hungry, and I loved butterbeans. I used to study about it. I wondered if what I'd done was bad enough to get that kind of whipping for."

Mary and her five children (Hicks was thirteen, Claude was eleven, Lilly nine, Clara Bell seven, and Ollie five) lived on at the hotel for a few weeks. Mary was pregnant. After the baby—Maggie Dorthy—was born they moved. Mr. Claude said, "We had to get some place where we could farm. We couldn't make a living at the hotel. We just went off and left it. We couldn't get nothing out of it. Nobody wanted to buy a run-down hotel in a town that was almost dead."

They moved to an old house in Anderson County, on land

[15]

that had at one time belonged to Mary's father, Madison Phillips, and that now belonged to her brother Amzy. Amzy came with a wagon and team to get them and their few belongings. This was the first time Claude had seen Amzy. He liked him.

Chapter 3

With Mary going around shut up in her own world of grief, with Hicks sick, and with Lilly determined not to work in the field, eleven-year-old Claude felt the burden of the family heavy on his own shoulders.

He knew how to farm. He'd worked on the farm most of his short life. Clara Bell was seven years old now, and she was willing to work, willing to try anything her big brother asked her to do. But they'd have to have a plow, and an ox or something to pull it.

As if in answer to their unvoiced need, Amzy arrived with an old mule he said used to belong to Madison Phillips. And he told Claude, "Come with me. I think I know where we can find a plow, and maybe a hoe or two, up here behind one of the old slave cabins—I saw them there awhile back."

They found one hoe that still had a good handle, and one without a handle. And there was an old Georgia stock that was partially rotted away, and three different sizes of rusty plowshares to go with it. Amzy said he would show Claude how to make some new wood pieces to repair the Georgia stock, and how to put a new handle in the hoe. They spent the rest of that day and the next fixing up the old farm tools.

Claude started breaking a plot behind the house, for a garden. Mary got some seeds from one of her sisters-in-law and she and Clara Bell planted them.

Amzy brought them an old one-horse wagon he said he didn't need any more, looked at the garden Claude had plowed, and allowed he couldn't have done better himself.

Claude started fixing up the rail fence around an old pasture, so they could turn the mule out to graze. One day a deer came running out of the woods and jumped the fence right where he was working, and Claude accomplished what he thought was an unheard-of feat by knocking it in the head with a piece of broken rail. A few days later when he and Amzy were visiting another uncle, Claude was relating the story with pride. The uncle said, "Oh, that ain't anything so uncommon. Every once in a while you hear of some feller knocking a deer in the head. When a deer's skeered it'll run into anything that gets in its way. More'n likely been some dogs chasing that'n."

Amzy said, "You ever knocked a deer in the head?" The uncle said, "Well, no, can't say as I have."

"Till you do," Amzy told him, "don't go talking down what this here boy done."

Amzy took Claude out in the woods and helped him catch four unmarked pigs. They decided on an identification mark for Claude and clipped the ears of the pigs accordingly. There were two males and two females. They castrated the males and turned the four loose. Amzy said, "Now, you'll have shoats to kill this fall, and next spring these two sows'll find pigs and you'll get yourself a start of hogs."

When Claude told Mary about the pigs she said, "Them pigs *belongs* to *somebody*."

Claude said, "Well, Uncle Amzy says if they ain't running with no sow, and if they ain't got no mark on 'em, they belong to whoever can catch 'em."

Mary said, "I want you to stay away from Amzy. He's gonna get you in trouble."

"But I like him."

"Ain't nobody said nothing about not liking him."

"It don't sound like you do."

"I ain't said I didn't *like* him. He's my brother, ain't he? Now you get out of here and stop bothering me, jest get on off out of here!" Mary turned around with a Dutch oven lid in her hand and Claude went out the door.

One of Mary's brothers-in-law, the one who was unimpressed by Claude's killing the deer, came bringing her six hens and a rooster. He said, "Thought I'd bring you some chickens and jest give 'em to you, afore you stole 'em, like you done my pigs."

Mary said, "People that's too lazy to mark they pigs *orght* to lose 'em."

"I got me a good mind to catch them chickens and take 'em back with me," the man declared as he stomped out of the house.

Mary and her children went hungry part of the time that spring, before things in the garden got big enough to eat. Some of their relatives gave them meal and a side of bacon, and when the weather got warm and the hens started to lay they had a few eggs to eat. But it was a hard spring and summer, was still hard the next winter. They killed the two male pigs, but they didn't make enough meat to last out the winter. Claude trapped, and when he'd catch a possum or coon they'd eat that. They even cured the meat of possums and coons, the way people cured pork.

Come the second spring, Claude started breaking the land again, doing a man's work from daylight to dark. Clara Bell was big enough to help a little with the plowing. She was eight. Mary worked in the field, too. Lilly stayed at the house to cook and take care of the younger children. Hicks sometimes felt well enough to do a little work, not much.

They were hungry that spring, too, just as they were the one before. All the cured meat had been eaten, and the chickens hadn't started to lay. They lived on corn pone and weevily field peas.

And to make matters worse, when Claude and Amzy went to round up Claude's hogs and mark the young pigs they found only one sow and three pigs. Amzy said, "Somebody done stole your hogs."

Claude could see another hungry winter coming up.

One evening when Claude came in from the field Lilly handed him a bucket and said, "The cow wants milking."

[19]

Claude said, "Well, go right ahead and milk her."

Lilly said, "I can't. I got to finish supper. Mama's gonna be mad if it ain't ready."

Claude said, "Tough." He sat on the steps and began whittling on the stock of a slingshot he was making.

Mary came around the corner of the house, and Lilly handed her the milk bucket and said, "Tell Claude to go milk the cow I can't leave the supper."

Mary handed the bucket toward Claude and said, "Here."

Claude said, "Milkin's not my job, and I ain't a gonna do it."

Mary whirled around and grabbed up a peach tree limb that six-year-old Ollie had been riding for a horse, and she started whipping Claude. She said, "Ain't no youngun of mine gonna tell me what he won't do!"

When Mr. Claude was old he used to talk about that. He said he wondered whether she was ever going to stop whipping him, said the thought crossed his mind that she just might kill him. But finally she stopped and sat down on the edge of the porch, exhausted, and said, "Now take that bucket and go milk that cow."

But the bucket was gone. Lilly was milking the cow.

When Claude was at his aunt's house one day, she gave him a cured ham to take home. He was afraid his uncle might be angry if he found out about it—the man had never seemed to like Claude. He asked his aunt, "Reckon you ought to do this?"

She said, "Go ahead and take it. It's probably from one of y'all's hogs, anyway."

Mr. Claude said that on his way home he got to thinking about how one of his sows had disappeared, and the other one had only three pigs. And he wondered about that, and about other things. Life seemed to be a game, and a person had to learn to play it, he supposed. He was tall and strong. And he had two good fists. He'd try to hold his own in the game.

In 1884 they were still living on Amzy's place. In spite of the fact that this was a period of general prosperity in Texas,

Mary and her children were barely able to feed themselves. That was the summer Claude was fifteen.

One day after the crops had been laid by, Amzy told Mary and Claude he had heard of a place over in Trinity County where they were hiring men to work on a construction job, grading a roadbed for a railroad. He was going over there and try to get work. He wanted to know whether Claude wanted to go with him. Claude did. And Mary reluctantly gave her permission.

It took them two days to walk to the place where the construction was going on. They were hired immediately. They lived with the rest of the work crew in a camp that consisted of several big tents where the men slept, and a cook tent presided over by one man who did nothing but cook.

Next to the foreman, the cook seemed to be the most important man in camp. One of the men tried to explain that to Claude. He said, "When a man's working hard he has to eat hard. And out like we are here, eating's about all the enjoyment a man gets. He damn well wants them eats to be good. A good cook knows he can be awful independent, and get away with it."

But Amzy wasn't accustomed to humoring a cook or anybody else. One morning he handed his plate of scrambled eggs back and said, "These eggs taste like sawdust."

The cook refused to accept the plate of eggs. He said, "Anybody don't like what I cook can cook his own."

Amzy said, "You're hired to cook my food, and I want it cooked right."

The foreman stepped up and stood between Amzy and the cook. His hand hovered over the revolver that hung at his side. Amzy glared at the cook and the cook glared at Amzy. Frying and sizzling noises began to come from the tent and the cook went back inside to attend to the food. Amzy threw his plate in after him and turned and walked off.

That night Claude wrote to his mother and told her about all the money he was making, but he didn't mention the altercation in camp that morning.

When the men were lounging around or eating, they sat on whatever they could find: logs, stumps, anything that was handy. Claude and Amzy had been working for two or three months when Amzy found a nail keg and carried it to camp to sit on. He considered it his private chair. One morning he came to breakfast and found a stack of pancakes on his nail keg. He roared, "Who put these damn flapjacks on my stool?"

The men, knowing the situation was potentially explosive, rushed up and helped themselves to the pancakes and cleared the top of Amzy's nail keg. But the top was now greasy. Amzy allowed in a voice that was meant to be heard he'd better not find flapjacks on his stool again.

The next morning Amzy and Claude beat everybody else to breakfast and found the nail keg holding another stack of pancakes. Amzy yelled for the cook to come out of that tent. He did—with a butcher knife in his hand. Amzy shot him—dead—and then took off.

Claude went home. And on his way he noticed a For Sale sign on a little sawmill that was near where he lived. He had money in his pocket. He would dearly love to own a sawmill. Unlike a farm, a sawmill would produce for him through good seasons and bad. A sawmill would make his dreams come true.

The man was willing to sell for what Claude could pay down and a small amount each year until it was paid for. So Claude bought the mill.

When he got home Mary and the girls gathered around him. He had never felt so loved, or so important. They had to hear all about the place, the work, everything. He told them, carefully leaving out a thing or two.

Mary said, "How did you happen to come home? Was the job done?"

Claude knew it would have to be told, sometime. He said, "Uncle Amzy shot a man, so I thought I'd better leave."

Mary said, "What'd I tell you? Didn't I tell you he was gonna get you in trouble?"

"I ain't in no trouble."

"Where's Amzy?"

"He got away. I don't know where he is."

"Well, I knowed he was gonna come to this. I jest knowed it."

Lilly changed the subject. "Claude, I sure am proud you come home. I seen the prettiest pair of shoes in the mail order catalogue. I ain't had no shoes since Papa died."

Mary spoke up. "Now, Lilly, you can do without shoes, like the rest of the younguns."

Lilly said, "Claude's got shoes."

"Claude's got to have shoes," Mary told her. "He can't set traps without shoes. Or work on construction gangs." She said, "I'm gonna need Claude's money to pay off that bill we owe at the store. And I've been thinking—if there's any left I might get us a cookstove. It sure hurts my back to be always stooping down to that fireplace."

Claude squirmed, and shuffled his feet, and picked at his rough hands. Finally he blurted out, "I ain't got no money."

Lilly said, "You ain't got no *money*?"

"What on earth did you do with all that money?" Mary wanted to know.

"I bought a sawmill," Claude said, weakly.

When Mr. Claude was old and living with Fred and Effie and their children he often talked about that mill. He said, "It was just a little old mill, probably like the one Papa had the boards for our lumber house sawed at. It run by steam. Used wood to heat the boiler. It didn't saw much lumber in a day. But it was mine, and I was mighty proud to have it."

He said, "I had to have somebody help me run it, so I hired some of my cousins. But that was a mistake. They was lazy, and I had to do most of the work myself. I'd work hard all day, then at night I'd have to keep the fire going under the boiler, so's we'd have steam to start sawing with the next morning. I thought I knowed what hard work was. But I didn't. Not till I started running that sawmill.

"It had a gristmill connected with it. In them days most sawmills did. That helped, because I took one-eighth of all the corn people brought to the mill, as pay for grinding it. That kept us in meal, and sometimes a little more. We tried to raise corn, but seemed like we never could raise enough to do us. We was always so hard up for something to cook that we eat up a lot of

[23]

ours while it was still roasting ears. Then we grated it to make bread after it was too hard for roasting ears. Come fall, we hardly ever had any left for meal. And we always needed a few ears to feed the hogs, to keep them coming in from the woods so's we could get hold of them when we wanted to butcher. We didn't need it for fattening them—they'd get fat on mast [hickory nuts, acorns, muscadines]. There was lots of mast in the woods then."

In addition to operating his sawmill, Claude tried to help Mary and the girls with the farming. Hicks was almost always sick. During the next few years their living continued to be hard to come by.

Mr. Claude told of an "awful drowth" in the spring of 1887, when he was eighteen years old. He said they had worked the ground up well that spring and got things planted early. Said Mary was happier than he'd seen her for a long time. She told them, "Things orght to come on, now, and *make* before it gets too hot, before the bugs gets to them too bad."

But the rain didn't come. "It was just terrible—we'd keep looking at the sky, hoping so hard we'd almost bust. There'd be clouds, then the next thing you'd know they'd be gone. The wind would come up, like it was gonna rain for sure, and the sky would get dark. But in a hour it would all blow over. The plants dried up while they was still little. Looked like it *tried* to rain but it couldn't. One time Mama got down on her knees and pounded her fists in the dry dirt there in the garden. That was a bad time."

They had to live on what Claude could make at the sawmill. He seldom got money for sawing lumber. What he got was one-eighth of whatever he sawed. And he'd have to trade that for what they had to buy, if he could. He said once he loaded the wagon with shingles and carried them all the way to Palestine and sold them for $5.00. He told his children, "Some folks, seemed like, had lots of money then. But I couldn't get hold of any, no matter how hard I tried."

In the spring of 1888 Claude took a bad cold that he was not able to get rid of. It was the worst cold he'd ever had. He couldn't stop coughing. One day when he was at the general store a doctor happened to be there, and when he heard Claude cough he told him, "Boy, you've got consumption. If you don't go someplace and take a cure you're gonna die." Claude asked what he meant. The doctor told him, "Go to Indian country. Them Indians know how to cure consumption. You go up there in Oklahoma Territory and them Indians'll cure you."

Claude went home and told Mary to sell his sawmill, and the next day he struck out for Oklahoma Territory—walking.

Chapter 4

Sometime in the spring or summer of 1890 Claude returned from Indian territory, cured of whatever had afflicted him, and started working for a man who was farming in the Wesley Chapel community, a few miles north of Crockett.

Mary and the other children were getting along fairly well on the farm. She had used the money she received from the sale of Claude's sawmill to pay off what they owed. They were far from well-off, but they were not going hungry any more.

By cotton-picking time that fall Claude was married to a fifteen-year-old girl named Liddie Luana Evans, and he and his bride were living with her father and stepmother in the Wesley Chapel community. Mr. Claude never talked of their courtship, but his children believe it was a short one. His son Fred says, "Papa wouldn't have been around for a long one. He wasn't what you'd call a patient man."

Liddie Luana Evans's mother died when Liddie was four years old, and she grew up in the home of her older sister Martha and Martha's husband, Jim Druitt, on a farm near Montgomery, Louisiana. In the summer of 1890 Liddie's father visited the Druitt farm and persuaded Liddie to come to Texas for a visit. And during that visit she met Claude Barr Kennedy and married him.

Although Liddie and Claude could go on living with her father's family, they wanted a home of their own. They bargained with the man Claude had been working for that they would pick cotton as payment for the lumber in a small house on his farm.

Claude carefully took down the house, marking each board so he would know how to put it up again at the new location. They picked cotton all fall, and finally they were ready to reconstruct their house. But two boards were missing.

When Claude told his employer about the missing boards the man said, "Oh, yes. I forgot to tell you. I needed two boards and I took a couple of the ones you had taken from the old house. I have some boards piled on the porch of one of them houses over on the other side of the farm. You can go over there and get yourself a couple of boards in place of the two I took."

Claude said, "Why didn't you go get two of them boards in the first place? Why'd you take mine? I had my boards all marked."

The man said, "Young man, this is my farm, and I'll damn well do as I please. If you don't like it you can go to hell."

Claude hit him.

The man was big. But Claude was tall, with long arms. And he was young.

A Negro woman cook came running and screaming. But Claude pounded the man up considerably before he stopped. Some teeth were knocked out, and one eyelid was torn and hanging down over the eye. The cook said, "You heard him tell you to go get them boards at that other place. How come you so mad about it? How come you hurt him like this?"

Claude walked over to the other house and picked up a couple of boards. Several farmhands were sitting on the porch where the lumber was piled. They tried to pass the time of day with him, but he was in no mood to be sociable. He didn't even speak, just took his boards and left.

A few days later Liddie's father came home from Crockett with the news that Claude's employer had sworn out a warrant for his arrest, for stealing lumber.

"I didn't steal no lumber!" Claude declared.

"They say he's got witnesses," his father-in-law said.

Claude remembered those men on the porch.

"You're in trouble," Liddie's father told him. "That man's got influence. Ain't nobody gonna take your word against his'n."

That evening as Claude and Liddie sat with the rest of the

family at the supper table a deputy sheriff rode up in the front yard. Claude went out the back door and into the woods behind the house.

That was the beginning of his time of running from the law.

Mr. Claude told his children that when he ran from his father-in-law's house into the forest, leaving Liddie sitting at the supper table, he was "scared half to death." He said he knew enough about the law to be afraid of it. He remembered that when John Holt arrested somebody, the person nearly always drew a prison term if a witness could be found who would swear he was guilty. And there were those farmhands, sitting on that porch. They probably thought he was stealing those boards.

As he ran deeper into the woods he tried to think of something he could do, tried to make a plan. And the plan he settled on was a natural one for him.

There were many big sawmills in East Texas at that time. After railroads were built into that part of the country in the 1870s lumber interests bought up vast acreages of the virgin-pine-covered land, and by the time Claude started running from the law in 1890 sawmills and sawmill towns dotted the area. Company stores flourished, channeling much of the money paid the workers right back into the coffers of the lumber companies. But to East Texans who had lived through the Civil War and its aftermath the opportunities offered by the lumber industry looked grand, and there was a general migration from small farm to milltown. A man who wanted to work could usually count on getting a job, if not at one sawmill then surely at the next. Claude decided to head for the milltowns.

A short time, maybe a week or two, after her young husband ran off into the woods Liddie received a letter. The agonies she probably suffered in the meantime are not known—the stories Mr. Claude told his children and grandchildren were from his own point of view. He said the letter contained some money and directions for her to get on the train and go to Trinity, and there to transfer to the Sabine Branch of the International and Great Northern going east, and just to keep riding un-

In the early days of lumbering, trees were felled by men with crosscut saws, which were kept sharp by a "filer" (man sitting in foreground). *Courtesy Temple-Eastex, Inc.*

til she was met by "a friend." Mr. Claude said he didn't sign the letter.

The Kennedy children sometimes speculate on the dilemma this letter must have posed for Liddie. She was a shy, quiet person. Perhaps she had ridden a train once before, when she came from Louisiana to Texas with her father. But this mysterious trip to an unknown destination must have been frightening for her. In any case, she followed the instructions in the letter and at Groveton, a town that had recently been carved out of the forest by the Trinity County Lumber company, Claude came on the train and took her off, to a home he had prepared for her.

He was working for the Trinity County Lumber Company as an engineer. That meant he worked with the engines and

Claude Barr Kennedy near the sawmill boilers (*foreground*). He was probably in his late thirties or early forties when this picture was taken. *Courtesy Effie Kennedy*

pumps and the boilers that made steam and furnished power to operate the mill. His experience with his own little sawmill had prepared him well for this job that was considered an important one at any sawmill.

Mr. Claude remembered clearly that first home he provided for Liddie, and often talked to his children and grandchildren about it. Although there was nothing but forest there when the Trinity County Lumber Company started operations in 1882, by 1890 a fair-sized town had grown up, with the mill and company-owned houses separated from the rest of the town by the railroad.

Claude rented a house in the mill district. He said it had four rooms, a back porch, and a front porch. And flush with his new job and the privilege of borrowing against his next pay envelope (when a man needed money he could go to the lumber company office and get a book of coupons that he could spend at

Row (company) houses of the type provided for the average workman's family in the early days of the East Texas lumber industry. *Courtesy Temple-Eastex, Inc.*

the company store, the amount of which would be deducted from his wages on the next payday), he set about to furnish his house.

He bought a cast-iron cookstove with four eyes on top and an oven underneath. He bought a tin heater for the sitting room, and to keep it from setting the house on fire he took a precaution that was customary at that time: he built a box about a foot wider and longer than the stove, put the box on the floor and filled it with sand, and set the heater in it.

[31]

Payroll office, with the bay window where the paymaster stood. *Courtesy Temple-Eastex, Inc.*

He built a dining table out of rough lumber and bought a piece of oilcloth to cover it. He got an iron bedstead and mattress and some straight chairs from a family that was moving. Then he bought a few pots and pans, and stocked the kitchen with coffee, sugar, meal, bacon, syrup, and dried butterbeans.

He refused to tell Liddie anything about the house until they got to it. That was a secret he wanted to spring on her. When he was old he liked to talk about that. He always said he didn't believe he ever saw her so excited as when she walked into that house. "She cried and cried, and said it was because she was so happy."

And Liddie had a secret of her own. She told Claude, "I

believe I'm in the family way." That sent him into ecstasy. And Liddie cried again, from happiness. He had a fine job, they had a nice home, and now they were going to have a baby. The fear of Claude's problem with the law was pushed far back on the edge of their consciousness.

They made friends with the next-door neighbors, a Mr. and Mrs. Tryon who had at one time lived in the Wesley Chapel community. Mrs. Tryon taught Liddie many things about cooking and housekeeping. They borrowed from each other sometimes—a cup of lard, a cup of sugar. And when they did they'd sit awhile in each other's kitchens and talk. But only in the daytime. Claude worked twelve hours a day, seven days a week, and when he came home he was tired. He didn't want any visiting in the evenings. He would, however, sometimes sit on the front porch with Liddie for half an hour or so after supper, just the two of them. Life was sweet.

Then one day Claude looked across the mill yard and saw a deputy sheriff talking with one of the foremen. He didn't wait to find out what it was about. He took off, in and around the mill buildings, and into the forest. He headed for the Sabine River and Louisiana, keeping away from the roads and railroads, striking a course through the woods. He knew if he could get across the Sabine the Texas lawmen couldn't come after him—they'd have to get the Louisiana lawmen to do it. And by that time he meant to be where they couldn't find him.

He escaped. He didn't know whether he had been followed. In fact, he wasn't even sure then that he was the subject of the deputy's conversation with the foreman. But he believed he must always be on the alert, that he must run first and ask questions later. It was a pattern he was to follow for many years.

In about a week Liddie received a letter and some money. She was instructed to get on the train and go to the Druitt farm near Montgomery, Louisiana, and stay with her sister Martha until "a friend" came for her.

Martha Druitt and her husband were settled, practical farmers, who had a comfortable home and an adequate income. They were glad to have Liddie back with them for a while, but

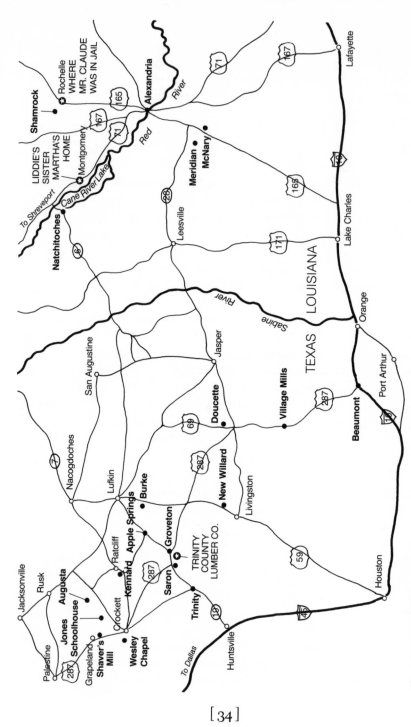

East Texas and Western Louisiana

they were distressed over the kind of life she and Claude were living. They tried to talk Claude into giving himself up and getting cleared of the charges against him. They believed he should be able to prove his innocence. But Claude believed otherwise.

Claude got a job at a sawmill near Montgomery. West Louisiana, like East Texas, was at that time dotted with sawmills and sawmill towns. A good workman could always get a job. He rented a mill house and gathered up some furniture. It was not as nice as the home they'd had in Groveton, but that was gone now. He told Liddie they'd have to make do for a while.

One day Claude came home and found Liddie crying. He had seen her with red eyes more than once, and he suspected she cried sometimes when he was away at work. She was heavy with child now. She told him she was afraid he would run away and leave her again. He gave her $20 and told her to keep it, not to spend it, so if he did have to go away she would have money for train fair to Martha's house.

She sewed the money into her petticoat and kept it safe.

They had been living in Louisiana less than a year, and had a three-month-old son, Horace, when Claude took off through the woods, running from the law again, this time heading for Texas. When it was clear that he was gone, Liddie ripped the $20 out of her underskirt and took her son and went to the Druitt farm.

A short time later she received a letter from her "friend," with money to pay for a train ticket to Saron, Texas. He had a job with the J. I. Cameron Lumber Company, and had fixed up another house for her. That was in the fall of 1891.

They had been living at Saron for several months when an engineer's job became available at the Trinity County Lumber Company in Groveton, and they went back there. They rented another house in the mill district and renewed their friendship with the Tryons. Liddie was pregnant with their second child. They were still living in Groveton when the baby was born, a son they named John.

Little John lived only a few days. Liddie and Claude were both distressed over losing a child, and for months afterward

Liddie cried every time the baby was mentioned. They had no way of knowing that this was only their first of many such experiences.

One day Claude looked up and saw a couple of lawmen walking toward him down the dolly run (an elevated system of wooden roadways connecting the various operations of the mill, and over which carts of lumber were moved, either by horsepower or manpower). Claude darted out of the engine room, jumped to the ground, and ran under the dolly run. The men called out that they wanted to talk to him, but he kept on running. He got away. But the men went to his house that time and talked with Liddie. They said there was a warrant out for his arrest, that a man in Houston County said he had stolen some lumber. They stayed around, watching for him to come home that night, but he didn't show up.

Liddie confided in her friend Mrs. Tryon. She said she was embarrassed that her husband was wanted by the law, even though she knew he was innocent. She said she was scared, too. Afraid somebody would shoot him while he was running, or that he might drown while swimming the river, or get bitten by a cottonmouth, or something. Mrs. Tryon told her, "Liddie, if you're gonna keep on living with that man, you're gonna have to somehow keep from getting upset every time he takes off like a hornet-stung mule."

Liddie took $20 from the secret pocket in her petticoat, got herself and two-year-old Horace on a train, and went back to the Druitt farm. She told Martha she felt sure Claude would be in Louisiana, someplace. Said, "Whenever he thinks the law's after him he puts the Sabine River between him and it as fast as he can."

She heard from him in a few days. He had a job at a sawmill near Natchitoches. He said the housing was poor, he'd do the best he could about fixing up a place to live, and would come for her.

The house was the worst they'd had. It was just one-by-twelve boards over a frame. Wasn't sealed on the inside. Didn't have glass at the windows, only shutters. When they first moved there the privy didn't even have a door, just had a piece of dirty

Lumber sheds at a planing mill. In front are the elevated wooden roadways, called dolly runs, over which lumber was moved in carts, either by horsepower or by manpower. *Courtesy Temple-Eastex, Inc.*

Mule hitched to lumber wagon, on dolly run. *Courtesy Temple-Eastex, Inc.*

rag hanging there. Liddie looked around and said, "These places ain't hardly fit for animals."

Claude told her, "You can see the neighbors is people."

She said, "Well, Uncle Jim's pigs live in better houses."

[37]

Martha and her husband came to visit and were appalled at the conditions under which Claude and Liddie were living. Jim Druitt took Claude for a walk down the railroad track and talked to him about getting a lawyer and going back to Wesley Chapel to try to find the Negro cook who had heard the man tell Claude to go and get the two boards he later accused him of stealing. Said he'd pay for the lawyer himself. But Claude believed the only way to stay out of trouble was to stay two jumps ahead of the law. He said the cook would not help him, that her sympathies were with the man she worked for, that she was angry because she thought Claude beat the man too hard. And Claude admitted he probably did beat him unnecessarily hard. Said, "My temper got away with me."

In 1895 another son, Francis Bell, was born to Liddie at the Druitt farm, while Claude was running from the law. He lived less than a week. Martha said, "Three younguns born and only one of 'em alive. It ain't any wonder that baby died—the way you've been dragged around from pillar to post."

Chapter 5

After Liddie recovered from Francis Bell's birth, and death, she and four-year-old Horace took a train to Groveton, where Claude was working at the time. When they transferred to the Sabine Branch of the International and Great Northern to go from Lufkin to Groveton they found it so crowded that Liddie had to hold Horace on her lap.

Most of the people on the train had been to a big affair given by John Henry Kirby, who had laid out the town of Kirbyville and was selling lots, establishing another sawmill town that was to become an important and lasting part of East Texas. There had been a free barbecue that day, and people were talking about a monkey that rode up in a basket attached to a balloon.

During the next few years Claude was restless. Either the law was trying harder to catch him or he imagined it was. He and Liddie and little Horace moved back and forth across the Sabine River, living a few months here, a few there, at many different sawmill towns. Once a sheriff's deputy cornered Claude by the millpond, and Claude threw the man in the pond and escaped.

Mr. Claude told his children he did the best he could to provide a comfortable home during that time, but the constant moving was hard on Liddie. He said, "I know she tried to content herself with the life we was forced to live. She was afraid if the law caught up with me I'd go to jail, guilty or not."

Once, after he had been running, he brought Liddie the paw of a large bobcat. He said he was walking through the woods near Natchitoches and looked up and saw a big bobcat on a limb just ahead of him. He shot the cat and cut off its four paws. He sold three of them in Natchitoches for $1.00 each, but he saved the fourth for Liddie.

In 1897 Liddie bore another son and named him Bruett. Like two of his older brothers, he died right away. He was born at the Druitt farm. Liddie did not even know where Claude was. In fact she was already having labor pains when she and little Horace reached Martha's house. This was the third child she had lost. But she refused to listen to Martha and her husband when they urged her to talk Claude into turning himself in to the law. She was offended that they spoke against him.

For a while that summer, life was better. They were back in Groveton. Liddie could gossip over the backyard fence in the daytime. Food was plentiful, especially fresh fruit and vegetables. People said East Texas was turning into a fruit- and vegetable-growing area. Oil was being pumped at Corsicana, and it was said that everybody was going to get rich. There were killings every weekend at the Old Doggie Saloon at Neame, and activities around the saloons in Groveton were not much better. There was plenty to gossip about.

By fall, though, Claude and his little family were back in Louisiana at another sawmill town.

Sometime in 1898 Liddie arrived at the Druitt farm with Horace in a high fever. He had had a bad cold and she had been doctoring him with mustard plasters and camphor melted in lard. In fact she had had a mustard plaster on his chest the night Claude didn't come home. She had bathed the little fellow and wrapped him in warm clothes and caught the train for Martha's house. Now he was very sick. Martha tried to doctor him, but his fever stayed high and he coughed all the time. They called the country doctor. He said the boy had pneumonia.

They didn't know how to get in touch with Claude. Because she didn't know anything else to do, Liddie sent a letter to him in care of the Trinity County Lumber Company, and it reached him. He got to the farm a few hours before Horace died.

Claude left Liddie at the farm for a while after Horace's death. He went to a little nearby sawmill town called Shamrock and got a job. He was working there when the law caught up with him and put him in jail at Rochelle, Louisiana. He couldn't believe it, couldn't understand how the lawmen had outsmarted him.

His stay in jail was short. He knocked a hole in the wall and escaped. Liddie received a letter saying her "friend" was in north Houston County, at the home of his sister Clara Bell and her husband, Charlie Allen. Liddie followed him there as soon as she could.

Clara Bell and Charlie owned a good farm near the Jones Schoolhouse community. They had several children, unlike Claude and Liddie who were now childless.

Perhaps Claude talked to Liddie about his escape from jail. If he did, she was the only one he talked to. It was purely by accident more than twenty years later that his son Fred learned his father had been in jail.

While Claude and Liddie were living with the Allens he rode a bicycle all the way to Ratcliff, about fifteen or twenty miles, where he worked for a company that was building the big Four-C Sawmill.

And it was during that time that he saw an advertisement in the Crockett newspaper, listing courses offered by the International Correspondence Schools. He enrolled in a course in electrical engineering. When he was old he told his children about that. "I was still taking the course a few months later when a mulatto from New Orleans, that had been installing the electric lights at the Four-C Mill, had to leave and go back to Louisiana because somebody in his family got sick. I got his job."

Mr. Claude said the management of the mill wrote to the International Correspondence Schools and asked whether they knew of anybody in East Texas who was qualified to finish installing the electrical system, and the school told them about Claude and assured them he could do the work.

Claude believed he could do it, too, and he went at it full of confidence. But when he got through and turned on the lights they didn't come on. He tinkered around with it and didn't say a word to anybody. He checked and checked but he couldn't find a thing wrong. It looked as if he'd done everything exactly right. But the lights wouldn't come on. Finally he gave up and went home. That night he lay awake, thinking, trying to figure out what might have gone wrong. And way up in the night it came to him—the main switch! He couldn't remember turning the main switch on. He got out of bed—they were living in Kennard then—and walked the three miles to the mill and flipped the main switch. The whole place lit up. He walked back home and slept the rest of the night.

They were still living in Kennard, and Claude was walking back and forth to Ratcliff, when their fifth son was born. This child, too, died in infancy. Five sons born, five sons dead.

Mr. Claude's children do not know when he and Liddie moved from Kennard, or why. Fred says, "Papa probably got mad about something at the mill and just walked off."

At any rate, in 1901 they were living in Groveton and Claude was working at the Trinity County Lumber Company again. That was the year their son Carl Atmar was born. He was named for L. P. Atmar, president of the bank at Groveton. And, unlike most of his brothers, this child was strong and healthy. He lived.

Groveton was becoming a thriving, important town. A large, two-story schoolhouse, with six classrooms and an auditorium, had been built. Segregation of the races was an unquestioned way of life in East Texas then, but the residents of the milltown were not segregated from people in the other part of Groveton. One school served white children from both sides of the track, while another school served all the black children. Churches also served people from both communites.

The talk in the saloons and over the backyard fences was

mostly about two subjects that year—the Mexican boll weevil that was destroying the cotton crop, and oil that gushed at a place called Spindletop. Neither of these was of much interest to Claude Barr Kennedy. He still worked from six in the morning until six at night, seven days a week, and when he got home he seemed concerned only with eating and going to bed.

In 1902 the people of Trinity County voted to prohibit the sale of intoxicants. It was now against the law to sell liquor. But that had little effect on saloonkeepers. They simply ignored the law. In December, 1903, a young Methodist preacher named Jesse Lee came to Groveton and started his famous war on the saloons. Groveton in those days was a rough and rowdy town. Women and children sometimes went hungry because men spent all their money in saloons before going home on payday. But Claude spent little time, or money, in the saloons. Heavy drinking was not one of his faults.

Also in 1902, Liddie bore another son. They named him William Claude, but they soon nicknamed him Curly. Like his brother Carl, this child survived.

In 1905 Claude and Liddie and their two little sons were living in Saron and Claude was working for the J. I. Cameron Lumber Company. On October 27 of that year another son was born. They named him Fred Wallace. This child was to become an important member of the family. It would be with him and his family that Mr. Claude would spend his last years, and it would be to him and to his wife Effie and their children that Mr. Claude would tell the tales related in this book.

Shortly after Fred was born a man from Trinity County Lumber Company persuaded Claude to go back there and work as an engineer.

When they moved back to Groveton they found that their friend Mrs. Tryon had a baby boy about the same age as Fred. She was complaining that her baby could not take all the milk she had, and she offered to nurse Fred as well as her own little boy. Liddie and Claude agreed to this because they thought perhaps the trouble with their babies that died was that Liddie's milk did not agree with them. Fred and the little Tryon boy both

Lumber company office, 1907. *Courtesy Temple-Eastex, Inc.*

grew strong. Claude and Liddie now had three healthy little boys—Carl who was four, Curly who was three, and Fred who was still a baby.

It was while they were living in Groveton that time that the superintendent of the Trinity County Lumber Company had a talk with Claude. He said, "Now, Claude, we know you must be in some kind of trouble. You no sooner get here and settle down than you up and leave, without notice. You are a good workman and we'd like to keep you here. If you'll let us, we want to help you. What are you running from ?"

Claude told him.

They sent the company lawyer to the Wesley Chapel community. He found the Negro cook who had heard her employer tell Claude to take the two boards, and her testimony was sufficient to get the charges against Claude dropped. Now, after fifteen years, there would be no more running from the law. But that did not necessarily mean Claude Barr Kennedy would settle down. Fred says, "Papa had a quick temper, and every time he got mad about something he'd just up and leave."

They were still living in Groveton, in a mill house, and Claude was working as engineer at the Trinity County Lumber Company's planing mill, when their daughter Alma was born in 1906, and their daughter Pearl in 1908. Both apparently were healthy children.

Two important things happened to Claude Barr Kennedy during the year of 1909, when he was forty years old. First, he went back to school. He always told his children, "I only got to go to school a little bit, two different winters." Just how much education he had received under the instruction of his father was never clear. It is obvious that he had sufficient background to study electrical engineering successfully at the time he installed the electrical system at the Four-C Mill around 1900. Of course the installation was not elaborate. It was for lights only— the mill machinery was powered by steam. At any rate, when the Trinity County Lumber Company offered night classes in English and mathematics he enrolled. He told his family he felt he needed it.

The second thing that happened to him that year was that he got whipped in a fist fight.

In those days fist fighting was a much practiced sport in East Texas. A good fighter commanded enormous respect. A fist fight between two men of acknowledged skill generally drew an appreciative crowd, and was the occasion for considerable betting.

Claude had done a lot of fist fighting when he was young. He often talked to his little sons about fist fighting. He'd say, "Get in the first lick, and make it count. But fight *fair*. And when you're through, no matter if you win or lose, be sure to shake hands with the feller you was fighting." He told them he had lost only one fight.

[45]

Fred says, "The way they done then, if it got around that a feller was good with his fists, why everybody else that could fight good would want to try him. But Papa had only been whipped one time. I expect a feller would have to feel like he was pretty good before he'd want to try Papa. I don't think he'd been fighting much for a good while. But this young man challenged him. I expect he was egged on by some of the men that wanted to bet on the fight."

None of Claude's family saw the fight that day. And that was just as well. Fred didn't know until after he was grown exactly what went on at that fight, and immediately afterward, but he knew his father stopped talking to them about fist fighting. Suddenly, that was a subject that was not discussed.

And Fred knew that the day after the fight Claude gathered up his family and left town.

PART II

This part of the story is told by Mr. Claude's son Fred, starting when Fred became old enough to remember. It is based on Fred's own memories and on Mr. Claude's reminiscing during the time he lived with Fred and Effie and their twelve children.

Chapter 6

Didn't none of us know nothing about the fight Papa had that day. I don't think Mama even knew, because she seemed mighty surprised when he came home and said to start getting our things together, that we was leaving Groveton. Said, "We're heading for Clara Bell's in the morning."

Mama didn't say nothing. She just set down on a chair and wrapped her apron around her hands and kept looking at Papa.

I was ready to go. It sounded like fun to me. But Carl didn't like it. He had friends he didn't want to leave. He said, "But how come, Papa? How come?"

All Papa would say was, "Don't you want to go see Aunt Clara Bell and Uncle Charlie and all them nice cousins?"

Papa had a little old contraption called a spring wagon. I think it was called that because it had a seat that was set on leaf springs, acrost the wagon, up front. Lots of people had them. Most people hitched just one horse to a spring wagon.

Papa piled our beds in the wagon, and what clothes we had. He didn't take the cookstove or the tin heater—I think he give them to one of the neighbors. He knocked the table apart and put the legs in the wagon. All we ever moved of our table was the legs. When we'd get to the new place Papa would just get some boards and make us a new table. But he always moved the legs.

Mama and Papa set on the wagon seat, and the two little girls set up there with them. Alma must a been about three years old and Pearl about two. Papa made a little place in the back for us three boys, on one of the mattresses.

When we got to Aunt Clara Bell's Grandma Kennedy was there. Grandma lived most of the time with her youngest daughter, Aunt Maggie, but she generally spént a few weeks every year with Aunt Clara Bell. I never knowed of her staying with Aunt Ollie, maybe she did. But I know she never stayed with Aunt Lilly. Papa said her and Aunt Lilly couldn't get along. Us kids was glad to see Grandma, even if she was always kind of cranky. Well, I guess Grandma was what you'd call bossy.

Papa started looking around for some way to make a living. He contracted to make a crop on what they called the Payne place, in the Jones Schoolhouse community, a few miles from Aunt Clara Bell's house.

I remember that house on the Payne place real well. It was a lot nicer than most of the places where we'd been living. I went back over there one time after I was grown, when I was visiting Aunt Clara Bell, just to see if it was as nice as I remembered. And it was.

It was a lumber house, a pretty common kind of house in that part of the country. Siding run up and down. Rough lumber. Twelve-inch boards with four-inch strips over the cracks. Sealed on the inside with narrow, beaded boards. It was set on pine blocks, cut square, sawed at a sawmill. Some houses was set on hand-hewed oak blocks, but this one was set on pine. For houses like that they would put pieces of two-by-eights or two-by-tens right on the ground, for footings, and set the blocks on those. They set blocks under all the sills, one block every eight or ten feet. The sills run around the outside edges of the house and under the partitions for the rooms. They didn't level the ground. They made the blocks fit the slope. At the house on the Payne place some of the blocks was maybe two or three feet high, some only about eighteen inches. It made a good place to play under there.

Mama went from room to room, kinda running her hand over things—along a windowsill, over a doorknob. The house even had a telephone, one of them boxes on the wall. Mama knowed how to work it. You had to turn a crank on the side of it if you wanted to call somebody. One long ring to call central [the

[50]

Houses in East Texas in the early 1900s were often set on wooden blocks or sections of logs. *Courtesy Temple-Eastex, Inc.*

operator], different longs and shorts to call the neighbors. Mama told us, "they have one of these at your Aunt Martha's house."

Mama and papa had both growed up on farms, but they hadn't farmed for a long time. Grandma said she'd better stay with us for a while and help them get started. Said she could cook and look after us children and Mama could work in the field. I don't think Mama had a chance to say anything about it. I think Grandma done the planning and Mama just went along with it without complaining. Mama didn't hardly ever complain about anything. But I expect she wanted to stay in there and keep that house herself—it was such a nice place.

Grandma looked after the house and us children, all right. But she done more than that. She was a workhorse herself, and she kept everybody else busy.

She made us gather sage grass and help her make brooms. She dripped water through wood ashes to get red lye, and she put that with hog grease and made lye soap. She found a piece of two-by-four that was about a foot long and got Carl to help her bore holes in it and put a handle to it, and she pulled corn shucks through the holes and made herself a mop to scrub the floor with.

She had Papa get her a two-foot piece of a oak tree trunk and she stood that on end and used it for a battling block when she washed our clothes. She'd soak the clothes in water and homemade soap, then she'd put them on the block and give one of us a paddle that she called a battle, and we had to beat them clothes. She called it battling the dirt out of them. Then she'd put them in a big old iron washpot there in the yard and boil them. Then she'd rinse them. I think lots of people done their clothes that way back then.

There was a plum thicket on that place. And Grandma made plum pies, plum butter, and plum jelly.

Pearl got sick. Mama and Grandma doctored her but she kept getting worse. They called a country doctor. When she died he said what killed her was a congested chill.

Mama and Papa thought maybe Pearl had swallowed a plum seed and that might a caused her death. I heard Mama say she wished she hadn't left us with Grandma, said she didn't think Grandma watched us any too close.

After the crop was gathered that fall Papa moved us to Shaver's Mill, a little ways out of Grapeland. He got a job there, hauling lumber with oxen. When he told us about the job Mama said, "Reckon you can work them oxen?"

Papa said, "Yeah. I can work 'em."

Uncle Charlie was there. He told Mama, said, "Claude *used* to know how to drive oxen." He laughed and looked at Papa and said, "Remember the time you liked to a whipped old man Tarr when he interfered with you and them oxen?"

Papa give him a dirty look and didn't say anything.

But Uncle Charlie went ahead and told the story. He said Papa was driving some oxen that belonged to a old man by the

Oxen used for hauling logs and lumber. Men drove them by snapping rawhide whips close to them, sometimes hitting them. *Courtesy Temple-Eastex, Inc.*

name of Tarr. Said the oxen went to balking on him, and he was working them over with a bullwhip. Said the old man came down there and was giving Papa a raking over about whipping his oxen. And Papa, he was all warmed up, with them balking and all, so he just turned on the man and went to work on *him* with that bullwhip. Uncle Charlie told Mama, "I guess that sent the old man to the house in a great big hurry."

I remember seeing Papa work oxen when we lived at Shaver's Mill. Remember seeing other men work them, too. They used them for hauling logs and lumber. They had a big lot there where they kept them at night, and where they fed them. These were six-, seven-, ten-year-old animals, great big old oxen. They'd hitch three pair to a wagon. Each man had one pair of what was called lead oxen. They went in front. They was trained better than the others, would mind better. The men drove them by snapping a whip around close to them, and sometimes hitting them. I think they had rope poppers on the end of rawhide whips. That would make more noise, and if you hit one with that kind of whip you wouldn't be so apt to cut it. Papa's whip had a handle on it about three feet long. He used both hands to hold it. He told me one time, "A man knows he's worked when he's drove oxen all day."

After Papa was old, when he was living with us, he told me about a thing that happened when we was living at Shaver's Mill, something I didn't know about at the time.

He said he was hauling a big load of logs with three yoke of oxen one day, and the weather was hot and the load was heavy. They was following up along a creek, and the oxen kept trying to go to the water to get a drink, but there hadn't been any place where he thought they could get down to it without upsetting the wagon. He said the lead oxen finally just broke out of control and went straight for the creek. The bank was high there and it crumbled some when they got to the edge. He got the other oxen stopped, but the lead team was too far up and they slipped over the edge and just hung there. They couldn't get back up. The only thing he could think of to do was cut them loose and let them fall into the creek. He thought it might break their necks. But it didn't.

We didn't have any toys. But we found things to play with. One day I was playing with a buggy whip, swinging it around holding the whip end and swinging the handle. Alma came around the corner of the house and the handle of the whip hit her in the head. She cried, of course, and I felt bad about hitting her. I don't know how long after that it was, but she got a earache. Didn't seem like anything Mama done for her made it any better, so they called a doctor. He said she had a rising in her ear that needed to be lanced. When he cut the inside of her ear pure blood run out. People said he was bound to a cut the wrong place.

Alma died.

I thought about the time I'd hit her in the head with the buggy whip, and I worried. Girls was something special. Now we didn't have no girls. I told Papa about hitting Alma in the head, but he said that didn't have nothing to do with her dying. But it kept coming back to my mind. I felt terrible. Papa must a guessed I was worrying, because he used to hold me on his lap a lot after supper. He didn't talk about Alma. He'd generally be

Sawmill boilers. A fireman is shoveling chips into the furnace. *Courtesy Temple-Eastex, Inc.*

talking to Mama. But he'd pick me up and hold me and let me lean against him, and I'd feel better.

When cotton was ready to gin that summer—somewhere around July or August—Papa left Shaver's Mill and started working for Mr. Worthington that owned a cotton gin in north Houston County. It wasn't far from Jones Schoolhouse. We lived in a house right there by the gin.

Papa's job was to fire the gin. He was the steam man. He

had to put the wood in the furnace and keep water in the boilers. He didn't do nothing else.

Four other men worked at the gin. It taken two men to tie the cotton out—tie the bales and roll them out of the way. And it taken two to work the stands. They had four stands all working at the same time. All four fed one press. The stands were actually the gins. That's where the cotton went down to the saws to get the seeds out. Fans fed it down through big pipes. The two men that worked the stands was called ginners. They used levers to adjust the amount of cotton going to the saws. After it went through the gins the clean cotton went over to the press and the seeds fell down underneath.

One day I stuck my head down in the press to see where the cotton was going. It was a automatic tromper, and when it came time for it to tromp down it came down on my head. One of the ginners happened to see it just in time. He reversed it and caught me. They taken me out there and put me down on the ground and poured water over me.

Papa was way back yonder with the boilers. He didn't know I was at the gin. I imagine I was lonesome, was why me to be bothering around there. I was the only child at home then. Alma and Pearl had died and Carl and Curly were going to school at Jones Schoolhouse.

While we was living at Worthington's Mill, Mama had her eleventh baby. It was a little girl. They named her May Bell. She didn't live but a few days.

Grandma had not been living with us for a while, but she came back about the time May Bell was born—to help Mama, I suppose.

Uncle Charlie brought Grandma, in a wagon pulled by a team of mules. After he left, Grandma said, "I don't know who's stubborner—Charlie or them mules."

Grandma, I don't think, liked Uncle Charlie a whole lot.

A man come from Groveton to see Papa. He come in a spring wagon, driving a great big workhorse. I remember he stayed all night with us. He wanted Papa to go back to Groveton and work for the Trinity County Lumber Company again. Said the company would get a house ready for us, and send a wagon to move us.

I suppose they wanted Papa pretty bad. I've heard men say what a good engineer he was, how he kept the equipment up, and how he could make a engine pull a lot more than the majority of men could. I know he fired the boilers and kept the engines up, both. I think when he wasn't there they maybe had to have two men doing that.

Papa went back to Groveton with the man the next day. I don't know what Mama thought about it. She was a person that didn't hardly look mad, or happy either. If Papa wanted to do a thing, she'd do it. She maybe was glad to move from north Houston County, though. We'd had so much bad luck there. We'd lost them three little girls.

Chapter 7

I think we might a all been glad to get back to Groveton. Us boys had other children to play with. And I think Papa liked working there at the lumbermill. He never did like to farm much. He'd do it if he had to.

I think Mama was proud to be back where she could visit with Mrs. Tryon. But I don't guess you could say she was exactly happy. I never heard her say anything, one way or the other. I know she pined for them little girls. She cut pictures out of a newspaper, pictures she thought looked like the girls—we didn't have no pictures of them. And she stuck them little pictures up on the wall in the kitchen. I'd see her, lots of times, standing there looking at them. She never said nothing, though. She, didn't seem like, was too terrible unhappy, neither. Mama just didn't show her feelings much, I reckon.

I remember her and Papa used to set on the steps of the front porch and sing old-timey songs after supper. We had one of them old wooden swings that hung by chains, there on the porch. But they didn't set in it. They set on the steps. They sung "Standing on the Promises," and "What a Friend We Have in Jesus," and "The Old Rugged Cross." And they sung "I Come from Alabama with My Banjo on My Knee"—that was one of Mama's favorites.

Us boys would be playing with the neighbor children, and Mama and Papa would be there on our steps singing. We didn't sing with them. I heard some of the other people around there singing like that a few times. But not as much as I heard Mama and Papa. They wouldn't sing very long, maybe half an hour. Papa always had to get to bed early.

We stayed up later than they did sometimes. If the weather would be good, and we'd be playing with other children, Papa would tell us, "You can stay out and play a little longer, but be quiet when you come to bed."

We'd play games like drop-the-handkerchief, or hide something. And sometimes we played what we called town-ball. It was a little like softball, but it just had two bases. We'd choose up sides and have two teams. Girls and boys both played. If the weather was bad, we'd go to some neighbor's house and play with their children. We never could invite children to play at our house. Papa needed his rest.

Sometimes there'd be some old woman, a grandmother or auntie, at one of the houses, and she'd tell us tales. About ghosts or something. Scare us half to death. And sometimes she'd be telling something scary and she'd jump at us and say *boo* and we'd about come out of our skin. Most grown-ups told children scary stores. Sometimes parents would say, "Old so-and-so's gonna get you if you don't be good." Try to scare children into doing what they wanted them to. Have them afraid to go in a dark room, or outside to the toilet after dark. Funny how you could go to them places in daylight and never even think a thing about it, never be scared a bit, but after dark you wouldn't go for nothing unless you just had to, and then sometimes the hair would almost stand up on your head.

I remember one time a colored man got hung. A white man killed his wife and children and laid it on the colored man and the people went and got him and hung him. Sometimes parents would scare their children by telling them this dead man was gonna get them. His name was Beeler.

One evening it was dark when we were eating supper. The house we were living in then didn't have no electricity, and Mama had lit a coal oil lamp so we could see to eat. Curly wasn't paying attention to eating, was just playing around, and they'd told him to eat up and he wasn't doing it. After while Mama picked up the lamp and took it in the sitting room, and left Curly there at the kitchen table in the dark. He said, Wait. . . . I ain't through eating my syrup."

The rest of us went in the other room where the lamp was. I guess Papa thought he'd have a little fun. He said, "Curly, be careful. Old Beeler's liable to get you."

Man, Curly came out of there. He was wearing bib overalls and he got his galluses caught on a nail in the wall. He commenced to scream and holler. He thought Old Beeler had him for sure.

People used Old Beeler to scare their children for a long time. They believed he really did murder that woman and children. But Papa told me years later that he heard that white man confessed on his deathbed. That other man was innocent. But the white man knowed he could get away with it. Wouldn't nobody take a colored man's word against a white man's.

People, back then, were pretty hard on colored people. Some of them probably deserved it. But some didn't. Papa told me about one time some white men rounded up a bunch of colored and hung them. I don't know what the colored had done. Killed a white man, likely. Or bothered a white girl. Anyhow, they got hold of several and hung all of them except one old woman. They knowed she hadn't done nothing, she was just with the others when they went to hang them. So they didn't hang her, they let her go. But in a little while she came back, said she was looking for her snuff box, said she must a dropped it there somewheres. The white men said, "You ought to a stayed gone." And they gathered her up and hung her, too.

Colored people have come a long way in my lifetime. When I was a boy seemed like the white people I knowed thought the colored was just a little above cattle—they was all right if you had some hard work to do. There was always some of them around the sawmills, but they just done the menial labor, didn't none of them have any of the good jobs. I never had any close association with any of them. We never had any of them working for us around the house. When Mama's health was bad Papa hired white girls to do the housework.

But, now my wife, her grandfather brought a colored man

and his wife to Texas as slaves, and the descendants of them people and my wife are good friends to this day.

Things have changed a lot since I was a boy. And that's good. It's as it should be. We have lots of educated colored people around here now. As nice people as you'd ever want to know. I guess some of them was nice all the time. I just didn't know it.

In Groveton, when I was about seven or eight years old I got one of the few whippings my father ever gave me.

Papa was in the habit of hiding his billfold under the mattress at night, and one morning he forgot to get it out and put it in his pocket. He come home to get it and couldn't find it. Mama told him I'd been playing in there.

When he caught up with me I had the billfold in my hand, trying to buy a homemade wagon from another little boy. Papa took me home and took his razor strap to me.

He talked to me a long time. He'd talk awhile and whip awhile. And he'd cry. He said, "You understand I can't let you do what you done. I've got to learn you not to do things like that." It looked like Papa couldn't hardly bear to whip one of us, he loved us so much. He should a whipped us more than he did.

Mama never whipped us. She'd slap us sometimes. She used to slap me if she caught me pinching the corn bread. She'd have the pan of bread setting there on the flour barrel, or on the back of the stove, while she got the rest of the supper ready. And if I went by there seemed like I just about had to pinch me a bite off the corner, where it was all nice and brown and crusty. I knowed if she caught me I was gonna get slapped. If Mama moved that left hand of hers you might as well not try to dodge, she'd hit you every time. But she never took a switch to us. She'd say, "I'm gonna tell your papa." But she never did, she acted like she forgot.

Papa didn't come home at noon, he couldn't leave the job. In the winter he carried his lunch with him when he left for work. In the summer, when we weren't in school, Mama'd get one of us boys to carry it to him fresh-cooked and hot, in a syrup bucket.

Children in them days went barefoot all summer. But I soon learned I had to wear shoes when I carried that lunch bucket over there. I had to walk the dolly run to get to Papa, and it had a lot of pine tar on it, and that tar was hot as fire. There was splinters, too, that the horses' feet broke loose. I didn't like shoes. But you had to wear them when you walked that dolly run.

One summer Papa bought me a pair of button shoes. I generally wore brogans—heavy shoes that come up over my ankles, laced up, had metal hooks at the top to hold the laces. All the boys I knowed wore that kind. They didn't cost much, and they wore like iron. But the company store must not a had any brogans that would fit me. They didn't get their stock of children's shoes in till up in the fall. More than likely them old button shoes was all Papa could get. They was probably something the store had had for years and couldn't sell. I suppose I'd done wore out my brogans, or outgrowed them. Anyhow, I had this pair of button shoes. I hated them. They was stiff as boards, and they rubbed up and down on my heels. And the other boys was always hoo-rahing me about them. So one day on the way home from carrying Papa's lunch I throwed the shoes in the millpond. Carl and Curly had to carry the lunch the rest of the summer. Papa took the razor strap to me that time, too.

We hadn't been living back in Groveton too long when Papa moved us to another house, one that wasn't a mill house. It belonged to a man he worked with, and the people that had been living in it moved from Groveton, so the man asked Papa if he didn't want to rent it.

It was what people called the old Wade place. It had lots of room. Had a upstairs. Mill houses rented for $5.00 or $6.00 a month, and I think Papa paid $7.00 for this one.

We was living in that big house when Papa's sister, Aunt Maggie, and her family came to spend Christmas with us. They brought Grandma. We had a big time. Mama made two cakes. She called them stacked cakes because they had several layers. White cakes and white icing. She never made chocolate cake.

And she made lemon pies. In the summer, sometimes, she'd make berry pies. But she made lemon pies in the winter.

Well, she didn't make no whole lot of pies anytime. Cakes neither. But she usually made some for Christmas. I remember she made taffy candy that Christmas, out of cane syrup. Her and Aunt Mag cooked a ham, and made chicken and dumplings. Mama never did cook a turkey.

What we eat, most every day, was dried field peas or dried beans—butterbeans was Papa's favorite—bacon or fatback, and corn bread and syrup. Sometimes she'd fry steak, roll it in flour and fry it. And sometimes we had fried chicken. For breakfast we had bacon and eggs, biscuits and syrup, and once in a while we'd have ham or steak for breakfast. Papa liked to eat well. Mama and Papa drunk coffee at every meal. Us children drunk water. We hardly ever had milk. Sometimes, if a neighbor had a cow, we'd take a syrup bucket and get a bucket of buttermilk. We didn't buy sweet milk. Mama made her biscuits with buttermilk if she had it, but mostly she made them with water. She never made bread with yeast. The only bread I recollect having at home when I was growing up was corn bread and biscuits.

We never paid no attention at all to birthdays. And we didn't pay much attention to Christmas, neither. That time when Aunt Mag and them was there was the best Christmas I can remember having. We never had a Christmas tree. Never got any toys. We'd hang our socks up on the back of a chair or something, and we generally got oranges and apples and nuts in them. Sometimes we got a shirt or something. I don't remember seeing any toys in the company store. And I don't remember any of the neighbor children getting toys. I don't believe they did. Looks like if they had I'd a wondered why we didn't. Some boys would make things, like the little wagon I was trying to buy the time I took Papa's billfold. That boy had sawed his wheels out of a round pine tree. But we never made toys. We didn't have nobody to show us how. Papa was always at work.

I don't know whether they had dolls in the company store or not. I know Alma and Pearl never had any.

Some of our friends had pets. But we didn't. Papa didn't want anything around to bother him. Somebody give us a puppy once. It was just a little thing, and it whined some the first night.

[63]

Papa said, "You better take that thing back where you got it. If it stays around here I'm liable to end up taking it to the mill and throwing it in the furnace." So we took it back.

Once when Grandma was visiting us, Mrs. Tryon come to set awhile and borry some vanilla. Mama climbed on a chair to get the vanilla from a top shelf. Grandma was a tall, angular woman. She looked at Mama on that chair and told Mrs. Tryon, "The devil owed me a debt and he paid me off in duck-legged son-in-laws and daughter-in-laws."

Mrs. Tryon said, "You better be careful or Liddie's gonna get mad."

Grandma said, "Oh, she never gets mad. She ain't got spunk enough."

Grandma was right. Mama didn't hardly ever show any temper. But I remember one occasion that proved she *could*. Our next-door neighbor was a woman almost everybody had trouble with. Mama hadn't had any run-in with her yet. But one day the woman's little girl come to our house to play on the porch swing. The little girl didn't have on no underpants. When Mama noticed that she told her, "You go home and put on some panties. I don't want you around my boys dressed like this."

That made the neighbor woman mad. She came out in the yard and started yelling for Mama to come to the fence and fight about it. Mama didn't pay her no mind. For two or three days the woman kept on yelling at Mama across the backyard fence. One day Mama was hanging clothes close to the fence, and the woman came and stuck her head over into Mama's face and begin to cuss at her. Mama reached up and caught her by the hair and held her with one hand and slapped her with the other. The woman went and called the law.

When the mill policeman came out that evening he told Mama and Papa, "That woman's had that coming for a long time. I just wish I could a seen it."

One day Curly and me got drunk. Papa always kept a bottle of whisky at the house. He didn't drink it. Oh, he might a drunk a little if he had a cold or something. I know he didn't drink

[64]

much, the same bottle would be there for a long time. What they used it mostly for was medicine for us children. They'd put a teaspoon of whisky and a little sugar in a glass of warm water and give it to us if we had a stomachache or something. I can remember saying I had a hurting in my stomach when I didn't, just to get a drink of whisky. We all liked it.

Well, one day Curly and me sneaked the bottle out and took it over to the lumber company pasture and had us a few drinks. I guess we had more than a few, maybe. I know that before I knowed it I was feeling sick. I told Curly, "We better go back to the house."

But Curly wasn't ready to go back. He begin to sing "I Come From Alabama." And he started dancing around. He was awful happy.

I wasn't happy. I said, "Curly, it's starting to get dark. I wanna go home." But I couldn't walk straight. And when Curly tried to help me he found out he couldn't walk straight, neither.

I begin to cry.

Then, there was Papa. He had come in from work and was looking for us. Curly still had the half-empty bottle in his hand, so Papa didn't have no trouble figuring everything out. He put the bottle in his pocket and took us by the hand and took us home.

He didn't even scold us that night. He told Mama, "They're not hurt—they're all right, they're just drunk." And they put us to bed.

Papa talked to us the next day. He didn't whip us. But he talked a long time. He said he didn't want us ever to do that again. Said it was beneath a person to drink too much whisky, made a person look like a fool. Said he didn't want his children acting like fools.

I think that was when they stopped keeping whiskey in the house.

When I was seven years old Papa started me to school. Carl and Curly were already going to school, and I'd heard them complaining about it. They didn't like it. I had made up my mind I wasn't gonna like it, neither. And I didn't.

[65]

School building with students and teachers, in an East Texas sawmill town in the early 1900s. This is probably the kind of building Fred and his brothers went to school in in most of the towns where they lived. *Courtesy Temple-Eastex, Inc.*

Carl and Curly and their friends played hookey a lot, and I tried to play hookey with them. Carl thought I was too young to be tagging along, and he would slap me and try to make me go back to school. I'd generally try to foller them, anyway, back behind a ways.

Most of the time they didn't do nothing special when they played hookey. They'd just carouse around, maybe get into somebody's melon patch or cane patch, if it was that time of year. Cane was like candy to us—we chewed it and sucked the juice.

But one time we all found plenty to do. The dam broke at

the millpond, and most of the water drained out. That left lots of fish stranded in the bottom of the pond. A bunch of boys—some from the mill district and some from across the tracks in Groveton—played hookey to catch fish. We could wade out in the pond and catch the fish in our hands. We sold them. The boys from the mill community sold theirs over in Groveton, and the boys from Groveton sold theirs in the milltown. We'd been doing that for several days before our parents found out about it.

Carl and Curly and me always carried our lunch with us to school, in syrup buckets. So we just carried it to the millpond. We didn't have no problem about that. We even went back home sometimes, to get something we needed, but we never got caught. We'd slip in and get whatever it was we's after. Mama'd be busy in the kitchen and never know we was there.

Finally the story got out, and Papa was mad. It was getting close to the end of school, anyway, so he whipped us and put us on the train and sent us to Aunt Clara Bell's and told Uncle Charlie to see that we worked on the farm. And Uncle Charlie done just that.

He put us to chopping sprouts out of his cotton field. We wasn't used to working, so I expect we didn't get much done. One day I was watching some geese he had there. He kept them to eat the grass out from around his cotton plants. They made funny little noises all the time. I thought they was pretty comical. Well, I got to watching them geese going up and down the rows, picking that grass, and I forgot to work. Uncle Charlie got him a switch and was tearing me up. Carl came up behind him and said, "You hit Fred another lick and I'll cut your head open with this hoe." Uncle Charlie stopped, but he said he was gonna tan both of us that evening. He did, too, with a buggy whip. I don't think he cut us. But he raised some mighty big whelts.

We was supposed to get another whipping the day Papa come to get us, but him getting there saved us. Grandma had come to visit Papa and Mama in Groveton, and when she found out where us boys was she sent Papa after us. She told him, "Don't you let Charlie whup them younguns, he whups too hard." Papa told me about it years later. He said he didn't say nothing back to her—she was his mother. But he thought to himself she didn't have much business talking about whipping somebody too hard. Anyhow, he came with two horses and a spring wagon and took us home.

Grandma was the onliest person I ever knowed that could boss Papa.

Papa generally had some horses around at that time. He was making extra money by buying up big, broke-down horses that had been used for moving lumber on the dolly runs, then fattening them up and selling them. He had put a tongue in his spring wagon so he could hitch two horses to it. He'd take them old wore-out dolly-run horses that he'd fed till they was fat and slick, and he'd train them—he'd hitch them to that wagon, and he'd use a buggy whip on them and every time he used the whip he'd pull hard on the reins. He'd get them to where all he had to do was tighten the reins and them horses would really get up and go. When a buyer seen how much life they seemed to have Papa wouldn't have no trouble selling them. I remember he got one of my uncles to carry some of them over in Louisiana and sell them to a paper mill for a pretty good price. It was probably a couple of them horses he used when he came to Aunt Clara Bell's to get us that time.

Chapter 8

One spring, another boy and me got to robbing birds' nests. We robbed every nest we could find, tried to collect as many different kinds of eggs as we could. We'd put them under a old setting hen Mama had there. She wasn't setting on any eggs, she was just setting. Hens are like that in the spring. They want to set on eggs, but if they ain't got no eggs under them they will set anyhow. We'd get birds' eggs and put under this old hen and she would hatch them. Then we'd take the baby birds and try to feed them bread crumbs.

I'd been noticing a old red headed peckerwood going in and out of a hole in a big dead pine tree out in the lumber company pasture, behind our house. We hadn't had any peckerwood eggs, so I told the other boy, "Les us go out there and see can we get us some peckerwood eggs."

He said, "Naw. That nest's too high up."

I said, "Les just go out there and see."

The tree was big. I tested the limb closest to the ground. It didn't break. I climbed up on it and tested the next limb. I went up pretty careful, with my arms around the trunk, trying not to put any more weight than I had to on the limbs. Dead pine limbs will snap off mighty easy. I knowed them limbs was liable to break with me.

I got up to where I could put my hand in the hole in the tree, and was just reaching in when the limb I was standing on snapped. If I'd had both arms around the trunk I might could a helt on, but I had that one hand in the bird's nest. I remember starting to fall, and trying to find something to grab onto. It must a knocked me out when I lit. I don't remember nothing about that. The boy said I hit on my head and shoulder and just laid there. He couldn't get me to say anything.

He started hollering for help, and a man that was walking acrost the pasture heard him and came and picked me up and carried me home and put me on the bed.

The man lived over on the other side of the millpond. I didn't know him, but I'd seen him around. I knowed folks spoke lightly of him, didn't associate with him. And I knowed why. It was because he lived over there close to the colored houses.

When Papa come he asked Mama, "How'd you get him home?"

She said, "That man that lives with the colored people carried him."

Papa said, "He did? That old man that lives over there on the other side of the pond?"

Mama said, "Yes."

Papa said, "Well, it don't make no difference who he lives with, this shows he's got a good heart."

My back hurt awful bad. Papa got the company doctor to come and see me. But he didn't do nothing for me. He didn't even examine my back, or give me no medicine. All he done was hoo-rah me about robbing birds' nests.

The company had this doctor there, just to treat the men and their families. It didn't cost nothing to have him. They took money out of the men's pay every month: $1.50 if a man was married, $1.00 if he was single.

The doctor had a little room there in one of the mill buildings, where he kept medicine and things. But he didn't tend to patients there, he went to their house. If you needed medicine he'd give it to you. It didn't cost nothing.

Well, them doctors wasn't much good, nohow. That one never did do nothing for me. My back hurt for a long time after that fall. He never come back to see me, never checked my back. I have wondered, after I got older, why Papa didn't carry me to another doctor somewheres. My back's been crooked ever since I fell out of that tree.

The next Sunday after I fell out of the tree a man came to our house. He told Mama he was a Church of Christ preacher. Said he heard I'd got hurt and he had come to see me. He was on his knees beside my bed, praying, when Papa come in from work. When he got through praying he got up and shook hands with Papa and told him who he was. They talked awhile and then Papa invited him to stay for supper. I think Mama was surprised. I know I was.

After the preacher left Papa said, "That's a good man. I like him."

Papa took to reading the Bible. He had always said the blessing before meals, kind of automatic-like. But now he'd read the Bible for a while after supper, and then he'd get down on his knees by a chair, and tell Mama and us to kneel down around him, and he'd pray. One day he told us he was fixing to join the Church of Christ. He said he had always supposed there wasn't any way for him to be connected with a church because he worked from six in the morning till six at night, seven days a week, "and the Methodists and Baptists expect their members to be at church twice on Sunday and every Wednesday night." But he told us, "This here Church of Christ preacher says it will be all right for me to come to church whenever I can, and not to come when I can't. And I'm gonna try to find some way to go to his church, once in a while."

The mill operated six days a week, so most of the men were off on Sunday. But Papa and a few others had to work every day. Papa used Sundays, when the mill was shut down, to wash out the boilers and clean the grates of the furnace, and make repairs.

He started having Carl and Curly and me help him with his work on Sunday mornings, so he could get through early and take off a few hours and go to church. He always took us with him. Mama didn't go very often, she wasn't in good health at that time. We didn't go to Sunday School, just church. We sat with Papa. There was other children there, too. I don't recollect

[71]

any of us making noise or any disturbance. Papa wouldn't allowed that.

In warm weather we wore just clean everyday clothes to church—bib overalls and blue denim shirts. And we went barefooted. But in the winters I can remember wearing short britches that bloused over my knees. They called them knickerbockers, or just knickers. We wore long cotton stockings. They was held up with garters Mama made out of plain elastic she bought at the store.

In the winter we all wore heavy cotton underclothes—long sleeves, and long legs that we tucked into our stockings. In the summer us boys wore underclothes that were lightweight, with short sleeves and short legs. But Papa wore the heavy ones year around. He said he wore them in winter to keep warm and in summer to keep cool. Said if he could get them full of sweat in hot weather he could stand it better around them boilers.

Didn't none of us have no heavy coats or jackets. We wore lightweight duck jackets. Us boys had heavy sweaters that buttoned up the front, and when it was real cold we might wear them under our jackets. But I never saw Papa wear a sweater.

Papa always wore a hat. A derby. But we wore cotton caps with bills. I wore one till I was twenty years old.

The only shoes any of us boys had was old brogans, except that little while I had to wear them awful button things.

Papa started reading the Bible at work. He rigged himself up a gravity oiling system, where the oil would drip on the machinery gradually and he didn't have to be constantly oiling it by hand. He would get it going, and then he could read his Bible for a little while. He got real interested in religion after he met that Church of Christ preacher.

We never had any magazines in our house, and the only books I ever saw there was the Bible and a old church hymnal. They took a newspaper part of the time. Papa read it.

Mama had her twelfth child in August, 1913. They named him Homer Alvin. Mama hadn't felt good for some time before he was born, and Papa hired a white girl to come and live with us and do the housework. The girl lived with us two or three

Skidder-loader, used to drag logs from where they were cut to the railroad, and then used to load them onto flat cars. This picture also shows horse and mule teams and some "big wheels," carts used for moving logs. The boys found the used coupons in such a skidder. *Courtesy Temple-Eastex, Inc.*

years. Her name was Allie. She could play the organ. I think she played by ear. Papa bought a old organ—the kind you pumped with your feet—and Allie would play after supper sometimes, and Papa and Mama would sing.

One summer my brothers and me and some of our friends found a whole bunch of used coupons. It was like finding money. The company paid the men every two weeks, but if you run out of money you could draw a book of coupons and they'd take it out of your wages the next payday. Some books was worth $1.00, some was worth as much as $10. They had 5¢, 10¢, 50¢ and $1.00 coupons in them. We found them in the furnace of a old broke-down skidder engine out in the woods.

The company kept these skidder engines on flat cars and moved them up and down the railroad track through the woods. They used them to snake logs in from where they was cut, and then they used them to load the logs onto train cars. The engine we found the coupons in wasn't being used any more. It was just setting out there by the track, rusting away. But they had been burning their used coupons in it. I guess that was a good place. Not much danger of the fire getting away from them. We saw a path going to the skidder is how come us to be looking around there. For some reason they had dumped a lot of used coupons in there and hadn't burned them. Maybe they had set them on fire and the fire had gone out. Anyway, there was all these coupons, and we helped ourselves.

When you was buying something with coupons you was supposed to hand your coupon book to the clerk and let him tear out the coupons that was needed. But lots of people tore out their own and just handed them to the clerk, so it wasn't anything uncommon for us to hand him coupons already tore out.

We bought all kinds of things with them coupons. But what we spent most of them for was to set us up a camp down in the woods. We bought dishes and knives and forks. And we bought nails and a hammer and a saw so we could make us a table to eat on. We bought a iron pot and skillet. And we bought lots of food. Bacon and eggs, syrup, beans, rice—stuff like that. We even bought a cast-iron cookstove. One of the big boys bought it, and was paying for it by the week to keep them from getting suspicious. He acted like it was for his mother.

We bought a baseball and bat, and some gloves. Baseball was important in East Texas then, so the company had lots of baseball stuff to sell.

We made us a flying jinny. We cut down a pine tree and left the stump sticking up about three feet. Then we shaved about six or eight inches of the top down to where it left a shoulder with a neck sticking up in the middle. Then we taken a pole and bored a hole in it so's it would fit over the neck that was sticking

The inside of a company store, early 1900s. *Courtesy Temple-Eastex, Inc.*

up. We nailed two-by-sixes on the pole to make seats. I don't remember where we got the auger and ax, but I supposed at the store. Anything we needed, we'd just buy it.

We'd go out there and spend the day playing and eating. Just boys. Wasn't no girls there. I guess this went on for maybe a month before the company found out about it.

A clerk got suspicious one day and asked to see the book of coupons a boy was using. So they caught the boy. And they was pretty mad. They said they was gonna prosecute him. They had the boy, and was talking pretty rough, when in walks his uncle who just happened to be in town, and happened to be a lawyer. When he found out what was going on he told the company

[75]

men, said, "No, you ain't gonna do nothing with this boy." Said, "It's against the law to use coupons in Texas now, and you know it. You bother this boy, and I'll take you to court for using illegal coupons."

So they let the boy go.

But that broke up our fun. They went out there and got all that stuff and taken it back to the store.

I don't think Papa knowed about it. I think maybe the lawyer told the company to just keep quiet about it or he'd sue them. Us boys talked about it some among ourselves. But Papa never did do nothing about it. That was one whipping we deserved that we didn't get.

Well, we deserved lots of whippings we didn't get. Papa was too good to us. He should a whipped us more. He'd whip us if he just had to. But it hurt him to whip us.

Chapter 9

In 1915 Papa bought his first automobile. It was a used Model-T touring car. He thought it needed to be tuned up, so he got his friend Cinch Ramey to work on it. Mr. Ramey drove the lumber company's motorcar, and it was a Model-T, so he knowed a lot about that kind of car. The motorcar was just a regular car except it had the kind of wheels that would run on railroad tracks. They had it to take the bosses out in the woods to see about the operations out there.

When Mr. Ramey got through working on Papa's car it wouldn't start. So they put me in there to steer it and they got behind and pushed. It started, all right, and just kept on going. The throttle on them Model-T's was like on a tractor, or a lawn mower. You just set it in a notch, at whatever speed you wanted, and it would stay there. You didn't have to do anything to it, it'd just keep going at that speed. They must a had it set faster than they thought, because it took off with me. I could steer it but I didn't know how to stop it. So I just kept steering. I went down the road and across the railroad tracks, into Groveton, up behind the grocery store and the bank, around the block, and was on my way back home when Papa jumped on the running board and jerked on the brake. It was fun for me. I guess it wasn't much fun for Papa.

My brother Joe was born that year. He was Mama's last baby. His real name was Clarence Edward, but we never called him that.

Cinch Ramey's name was Clarence Edward. And he had a son that was Clarence Edward but was called Joe. My brother was named for that boy.

Our Joe was a unusual baby. He was born already circumcised. Nobody we knowed had ever heard of such a thing. There was a lot of talk about it.

One day a Jewish peddler came and was trying to sell Mama some things. Every once in a while one of these peddlers would come through the country, going from one house to another. They had all kinds of things, like tablecloths and fancy pieces of cloth, baby clothes, and I don't know what all. I remember this one was driving a White Steamer, and I was more interested in the car than in the man and what he was selling. I was having a lot of fun looking that big car over when I heard a commotion in the house and went to see what was going on. The man had found out Joe had been born already circumcised, and he couldn't get over it. He said it must be a sign of some kind, said God had blessed that baby boy. He gave Mama a whole lot of things for the baby. Didn't charge her a thing.

Carl went to work at the lumbermill. Curly and me envied him. He had lots of money to spend. Papa didn't charge him any room and board. Never did charge any of us for room and board. When we worked we kept all our money and just wasted it. Papa thought he was being good to us.

Grandma was at our house in Groveton for several months in the spring and summer of 1916. She was sick. For one thing, she had a broken hip. But she had other things wrong with her, too.

I used to pick at her sometimes when she'd be setting in her chair, and she'd hit at me with her crutch. She would a hit me, too, if she could. I shouldn't a done it. But it seemed funny to me then, to see her get mad. Sometimes I'd act like I was gonna take her letters she got from Aunt Mag or Aunt Clara Bell, and she'd get fighting mad. She could read and write. She didn't wear glasses. That didn't seem strange to me then, but when I look back on it now it seems unusual, for a person her age. She was seventy-five.

She was bedfast for a good while. Mama had to wait on her. We didn't have the hired girl then because Mama's health had got better. Mama carried the slop jars, washed the soiled bedclothes. She washed in a galvanized tub, with a rub board. In warm weather she washed in the back yard, but I have seen her have the tub in the kitchen when it'd be cold outside. We had cold running water coming out of a faucet in the wall in the kitchen. No hot water except what she heated on the cookstove. Didn't have no sink. She throwed the washwater and the dishwater out the back door, just out in the yard. Had a outside toilet.

I know it must a been hard on Mama, having Grandma there that way. They should a made us boys help, but they didn't. Mama done it all. Papa's sisters would come sometimes and stay a week or so, and they'd help. But when they come they brought their children. There'd be three or four, maybe. Us kids would sleep on pallets on the floor so the grownups could have the beds.

Grandma died in July. They put her coffin in a wagon and took her to Parker Cemetery, near Jones Schoolhouse, close to Aunt Clara Bell's house, to bury her. That's where Alma and Pearl was buried. We had the Model-T then, but I suppose they couldn't get the coffin in that, is why they taken the wagon.

A man Papa didn't know come and talked to him at Grandma's funeral. He said he knowed Grandma when she was young. He knowed her brother Amzy, too. Papa hadn't seen Amzy since the time he shot that cook and took off running. He'd heard that Amzy was down around Apple Springs one time, working for a farmer down there. They said he'd been in prison for a couple of years but had got out on good behavior. None of the family had heard from him. They didn't know what happened to him. But this man at Grandma's funeral said he heard that Amzy went to Oklahoma Territory and married a Indian. Papa told Mama and us about talking to the man. Then he talked about that time he saw Amzy kill the cook. He said, "I always liked Uncle Amzy. He was good to me."

Just before Christmas that year Papa got drunk. He wasn't a drinking man, but he got drunk that time.

On Christmas Eve one of his friends talked him into driving him to Westfield to take a Christmas present to the feller's girl. The man had a bottle, and by the time they started back home him and Papa was both drunk. Papa run the car into a ditch and bent one of the radius rods. That was easy to do in them old Model-T's. It is a wonder they ever got back to Groveton. But they did. And Papa lost control of the car again and run it up in a man's yard, tore down the fence. The man come out and wanted to know what Papa thought he was doing, and Papa give him a cussing.

The man slipped out the back way and got the law to come. When they found out how drunk Papa was they took him and put him in jail.

Mama didn't do nothing about it. Papa stayed in jail all night. By morning he had sobered up, so they let him come home. That was Christmas day.

Papa was so embarrassed he never even went back to the job. We just packed up and left town, and went to Aunt Clara Bell's.

I don't think Mama told Aunt Clara Bell about Papa being in jail. I never heard her quarreling at him about it, neither. They didn't hardly ever argue with each other about anything. They got along good. But I know Mama give him his way.

We stayed with Aunt Clara Bell and her family for several days, and then Papa loaded us in the Model-T and took off for Trinity.

Them old East Texas dirt roads was always muddy and bad in the winter. We got down pretty close to Trinity and got stuck in a mud hole. The car sunk down to the axle.

It was awful cold. And it begin to snow.

There was a family living in a tent right close to where we got stuck, and we all went in the tent with them. I guess we must a stayed there in that tent with that man and his wife and children for two or three days. Slept with blankets on the ground. There was seven of us besides that other family, but I don't recollect it being too crowded. We stayed in the tent, we didn't stay outside, it was too cold. It come a big snow, and a freeze.

Them people must a been from up north somewhere, because they said they was used to snow. The children showed us how to tromp paths in the snow and play fox-and-geese. That snow was the prettiest sight. It covered up everything. I'd never seen anything like it. But the next day the sun come out and it begin to melt.

I don't know whether Papa knowed the people in the tent before or not, but I don't think he did. I reckon he just talked to the man and he told us to come on in. There wasn't any houses around there. I don't know how come them people to be living there in that tent. Maybe they was traveling, like us, and had to stop on account of the bad weather.

Papa got the car unstuck and we went on into Trinity. Papa and Carl got jobs at the mill there and we moved into a mill house. I don't know what happened to the people in the tent.

The mill was shut down for some reason. But they had to keep up steam for insurance purposes, and they needed some wood for firing the boilers. So they got Papa and Carl to cut some red-heart, or doty-heart, trees. That was trees with a decayed heart.

Then they decided to get Papa to help them put in a wooden water line from the mill to the Trinity River. They made the line by nailing four one-by-four boards together, boxing them together. I don't know exactly how they made it watertight, maybe they used pine tar. They pumped the water from the river to the mill through that line.

We didn't stay in Trinity but a few weeks. Then we went to a place called Doucette, a sawmill town north of Woodville. We went on the train. Papa sold his car. He'd had enough of them winter roads.

After we got to Doucette he decided to buy another second-hand Model-T, and he needed $100. He worked every day and he couldn't get off to go to the bank, so he sent Carl. Sent him to Groveton to Mr. Atmar's bank.

The clerks in the bank didn't know Carl, didn't know he was Carl Atmar Kennedy, named for Mr. Atmar. So when he walked in there and said he wanted to borry $100, his daddy sent him to borry $100, they just laughed at him. They wasn't thinking about letting that boy have no money. Mr. Atmar heard them laughing and come to see what was going on. They told him, "This here boy wants to borry $100, says his daddy wants to buy a car."

Mr. Atmar said, "Well, whose boy is he?"

Carl said, "I'm Carl Kennedy, Mr. Atmar."

Mr. Atmar said, "Well I declare! Carl Atmar Kennedy! Claude's boy."

Carl said, "Yes sir."

Mr. Atmar told the clerks, "Let him have what he wants."

So they gave him the $100. I don't think he even had to sign anything, they just put it down in the book.

We hadn't been in Doucette quite a year when we left there and went to Village Mills, another sawmill town, between Woodville and Beaumont. I think Papa got a little more money is why we moved. I don't know just how much he was making there, but he was making $90 a month when we left Groveton. We only stayed at Village Mills two or three months.

We moved to a little place in Texas called Carmel, a few miles from Beaumont, and stayed there two or three months. A man Papa had knowed in Groveton come and got him to go to Carmel. That was during World War I. I had my first job there. I was thirteen years old. I made a man's wages—30¢ a hour. I fed what they called a fuel hog. That was a big iron outfit that had six-inch iron blades. Them blades chopped lumber up into chips about half a inch thick and maybe two or three inches square, and that was what they fired the boilers with.

What we fed the fuel hog was slabs that come from the saws, the part with the bark on it that they cut off before they started to saw the lumber. There was a trough that carried the slabs down where the blades were. The sawyers would cut the slabs into four-foot lengths and take out everything that would make a two-inch lath. The rest of it come down a belt and another feller and me picked it up by hand and throwed it down the trough into the fuel hog.

Carl and Curly were working at Carmel, too. That made four of us working. Flour and sugar was rationed then, but we got plenty of it because when a employee went to buy it they'd ask you how many was in your family and let you have enough for that many people. Each one of us could get enough for our whole family.

Hadn't none of us been going to school since we left Groveton. I guess we was moving so much Papa didn't see any use in trying to put us in school.

We moved from Carmel to Beaumont and Papa went to work at the old Crosby Hotel, as chief engineer. They had oil burners and made steam for cooking and heating. He run the boilers. He made ice, too. And ice cream. And while we was there Papa invented a mechnical refrigerator that run on coal oil. He never did get nothing out of it. He just invented it. He didn't know how to get a patent for it, or how to get it manufactured and sold. He talked about that after he got old. He said he invented a railroad switch, too. Never got nothing out of it, neither. He said he wished he'd a knowed how to take advantage of what he done. Said it might a made him rich.

Papa started me to school in Beaumont. I went to a nice big brick building. But I didn't get to go too much. Carl got sick and Papa took me out of school to help Mama take of Carl, and to run errands and tote medicine.

We was living in Beaumont when the war ended.

In 1920 we moved from Beaumont to McNary, Louisiana. That's where I learned to drive cars. Papa had traded his old Model-T for a Maxwell, and I learned on that. I had me a regular business going—I washed people's cars. Spring Creek was a mile and a half away, and it had a rock bottom. That made a good place to wash cars. I'd drive a car down there and wash it. I had to be careful—cars had different kinds of transmissions then. Some had Yale shifts and some had standard shifts. And then there were the T-Models. I'd get in a car and ease it into gear and feed it just a tiny bit of gas and see which way it would go. I never did wreck nobody's car.

Papa was in charge of the boilers and engines at the planing mill there at McNary, and Carl and Curly were working at the mill. A planing mill is where the lumber is dressed. Some places where he worked Papa would be at the sawmill, and some places he'd be at the planing mill. They had different boilers but they were always pretty close together, on the same grounds.

We didn't stay at McNary but a few months. Left because Papa had a run-in with the boss. Lots of times when we'd move I wouldn't know why. But I knew how come us to leave McNary.

They were going to put some pipes together to connect some boilers and they needed a elbow they didn't have, so Papa decided to bend a piece of pipe. Wasn't too many people knowed how to bend them pipes. You had to put sand in them and get the pipe good and hot before you tried to bend it. I think they used some kind of heating torch. Anyway, the boss come down there and he didn't understand what was going on. He said, "Stop! You're gonna ruin that pipe!"

Papa got a hammer after him and run him off. Then he went ahead and bent the pipe and connected the boilers.

Then we left McNary.

Chapter 10

Papa got a job at Meridian. It was only a few miles from McNary, so we didn't have to move very far that time. It was the best job he ever had. He made $200 a month. It was a tolerable new sawmill, and Papa was chief engineer. We stayed there about a year and a half.

While we were living there Papa took Alvin to Alexandria and had his tonsils and adenoids taken out. They went on the train. I think they were just gone one night. Mama stayed with us.

All three of us older boys worked at the mill in Meridian. I fed the fuel hog. Made 30¢ a hour, same as I made at Carmel.

One time I almost got into trouble. One of the bosses come over there and told me, "Don't let any of them slabs get away from you. Throw everything that comes down that belt into the hog, we're getting low on fuel." So when a eight-by-eight about seven feet long come along I caught one end of it and heaved it into the trough going to the hog. They didn't mean for me to do that. That thing had accidentally got off the slasher table and onto the belt. When I throwed it into the hog it knocked the belt off, and they had to stop the mill and get it back on. They told me not to do that no more.

Papa put me back in school that fall. I guess I went about two or three weeks before I got myself in a scrape.

There was a place out in the woods they called the Camp, where a bunch of loggers and their families were living. And a little carnival had set up out there. One morning I decided to play hookey and catch the train down to the Camp and go to the carnival. The train left out at seven in the morning and came back at noon. I didn't think nobody'd know I went.

Well, the mill foreman happened to be at the depot that morning and he seen me leave. He went and told Papa, said, "If Fred's not gonna go to school I can put him to work, I need a hand."

So Papa got down the old razor strap that night and he told me, "You can do either one you want to—you can go to school or you can go to work." So I went to work. I guess I thought about all the money I'd have. I never went to school again.

We worked six days a week, eleven hours a day. That comes to $19.80 a week. I don't know what I done with all that money. Just wasted it. I think when I was working I bought my own clothes. I don't remember buying anything for anybody else, don't remember buying my mother anything. Oh, maybe when I went to a carnival I'd win a doll, that you could put a light in her head, and I'd take that to Mama. When there wasn't a carnival there I spent my money at the company store. And there was a picture show, I went to that. I wasn't going with girls then.

I guess I worked about a year there at Meridian, feeding the fuel hog. But I finally caused Papa to lose his good job there.

The saws shut down for a few minutes about ten o'clock every morning and I wouldn't have nothing to do for a little while. I'd generally go over to the company store and get me a candy bar or something. One morning I run over there and hurried up the six or eight steps, in a sweat to get my candy bar in time to eat it before the saws started up again. The store porch was stacked with boxes of supplies that had been delivered that morning. Just as I was hurrying along the clear space a colored boy come out the door and started for the steps. I expected him to step back and let me pass but he didn't do it. So I knocked him off the porch. It was several feet down to the ground.

The superintendent of the mill happened to be in the store, and he seen what happened. He got on me for knocking the boy off the porch. I had learned to cuss pretty good by then, so I give the man a cussing and called him a nigger lover. He went and told Papa I'd have to leave, he didn't want me around there no more.

Mama's brother, Ben Evans, was living and working at one

Woods camp, early 1900s, similar to that where Fred lived with his Uncle Ben Evans. The box-car houses that families lived in could be set on flat cars and moved by train from camp to camp. *Courtesy Temple-Eastex, Inc.*

of the camps out from a sawmill near Meridian, so Papa sent me to stay with Uncle Ben and his family. I stayed down there for a few weeks and I got tired of that. I didn't have no job, didn't have no money. There wouldn't a been any place to spend it if I had—wasn't any picture show, wasn't even a company store. So I just went back home.

The superintendent got the mill police after me. He said I had to leave. Papa said there wasn't no law said a boy couldn't stay at his home.

The superintendent fired Papa.

When we left Meridian we went to Shamrock, a little saw-mill town about four miles from Rochelle, north of Alexandria.

Carl didn't go, he kept on working at Meridian. We didn't stay very long. Papa just went up there to do a special job.

This wasn't the first time Papa had worked at Shamrock. But didn't none of us boys know that. We didn't know we was gonna find out something important about our father. We just thought this was another one of them temporary moves to a sawmill town. We'd seen a lot of them.

The mill at Shamrock had been sawing pine, and instead of burning chips in the furnaces they had been burning pine sawdust. Now they were going to saw hardwood and they wanted to burn hardwood sawdust. Hardwood dust was harder to burn, you had to have blowers to make it burn. So Papa was brought up there to put the blowers in. He could do different things like that, that other men, seemed like, couldn't do.

He run quarter-inch pipes from the boilers to the furnaces, to carry steam. After they'd get the furnaces going and get up a little steam, they could open the pipes and blow steam under the grates and make the sawdust burn hotter. That old sawdust was wet anyhow, the steam didn't make it too wet to burn. If it got hot it'd burn. They could a done the same thing with compressed air but they didn't have that, and they did have steam. They were burning hardwood sawdust to make the steam, and using a little bit of the steam to come back and make the sawdust burn.

After Papa got through installing the blowers, they got him to change a couple of train engines from pine-knot burners to coal burners.

They didn't have no house for us when we first went to Shamrock, so we had to stay in the old company hotel for a week or so. We had two rooms. Wasn't nothing in them but a iron bedstead and a washstand with a pitcher and a washpan. We had to go downstairs and out behind the building to get to the privy. We ate our meals in the dining room, where everybody ate at one long table, family style. We didn't like the food. I remember how glad we was when they finally got a house for us and Mama could cook us some beans and bacon and corn bread.

The house they give us wasn't much more than a shack but we moved into it, with what furniture we'd brought with us. We

Lumber company hotel, or boarding house, early 1900s. Fred and his family lived in a place like this when they first moved to Shamrock. *Courtesy Temple-Eastex, Inc.*

knowed we wouldn't be there long, so we didn't put up curtains or anything. We was just kind of camping.

After Papa finished installing the blowers and changing the engines he was through. He left us in Shamrock while he went looking for another job. He told me, "I'm gonna have to trust you to take care of Mama and the other boys. You're younger than Curly, but you're more growed-up than he is." He give me three $20 bills and told me to be careful not to lose them. He said, "You'll have to buy groceries and things, and you'll have to hire somebody to move our furniture to the train in Rochelle when I find a job." That was in 1921. I was sixteen.

[89]

One day when I was buying groceries at the company store I was out of change and had to break a $20 bill. The groceries didn't come to more than $2.00 or $3.00. The clerk handed me change for $10. I said, "I give you a $20 bill."

The man said I hadn't, said I'd give him a $10 bill. I argued with him, but he stuck to his story. Even offered to allow me to check the cash drawer, said, "See here. There ain't no $20 bills in here."

I knowed he was lying. I knowed I'd give him $20. I told him, "I'm gonna go home and get my gun and you're gonna find that $20." And I picked up my groceries and left.

Well, almost before I got to the house that man was there, apologizing, and handing me $10. Said he found the $20 bill, that he had put it in his vest pocket instead of in the cash drawer. I always suspicioned he knowed what he was doing all the time.

That night somebody tried to open the locked door of our house. It wasn't a very good door. It just had one of them little thumb locks. I guess whoever was trying to open it didn't try very hard. The lock held.

Later that evening somebody started flashing a flashlight in our windows. They'd shine it in, then they'd wait awhile and shine it in again. We blowed out the coal oil lamp and set there in the dark. Without any curtains or blinds we didn't have no place to hide.

I got me a piece of stovewood and opened my penknife. And every once in a while that light would shine in one of the windows. They were trying to see what we was doing, I reckon. It was pretty scary. We didn't have no gun—I'd just *said* I had a gun.

About midnight I'd had enough of that. I handed my piece of stovewood and my knife to Curly, and I run out the back door to a neighbor's house to borry a shotgun. The man give me the gun and told me, "Shoot a hole through 'em you can jump through."

We didn't go to bed that night, just set there, scared. We never did know who was flashing that light. But I always wonderd about that clerk at the store. He probably saw I had some money. It wouldn't a been too unusual for me to a shot him if he had robbed me. That was the way people stood up for their rights.

Papa got a job at the Long Pine Lumber Company at Alexandria, Louisiana, and rented a house. He sent word for Curly and me to crate up our furniture and help Mama move. My older brothers and me always had to crate the furniture when we moved. We generally moved by train and everything had to be crated. We got mighty tired of that. Papa would be done gone ahead to get a job and see about us a house.

I hired a man with a wagon and team to haul the furniture to the depot in Rochelle. A neighbor took Mama and Alvin and Joe in a buggy, but Curly and me rode on the wagon with the furniture. And when we was driving through Rochelle on that wagon I saw something I couldn't believe.

There was a old brick jail over there, with a big hole in the wall, and up above the hole it said, "Claude Barr Kennedy." I said, "Curly, looky there! What does that mean?" Curly didn't know. But we both begin to get mighty curious. And when Mama got to the depot we asked her about it. All she would say was, "You'll have to ask your Papa." And of course as soon as we got a chance we done just that. We asked him. And he told us. It was the first time any of us boys had heard the story.

He told us about his trouble with the man that said he stole them two boards, and about all them years of running from the law, and how Aunt Martha and Uncle Jim tried to get him to give himself up. He said he was careless, was why the law could catch him. Said he didn't expect them to find him in Shamrock that soon. Said he didn't know until years later that Aunt Martha and Uncle Jim had told the law how to catch him.

But he said he didn't stay in jail very long. Said he made friends with the jailer's wife. She brought his meals, and she brought him newspapers to read. He told her he was innocent, and she acted like she believed him.

One day she caught him working the mortar out from between the bricks in the outside wall of his cell. He said he cried, and played on her sympathy. Said she told him, "Well, if you're planning to escape, this evening would be a good time. We'll all be down at the river—we have a shipment of supplies coming in."

So he broke out of jail and headed for Aunt Clara Bell's in East Texas.

Curly and me thought that was the most exciting story we'd ever heard, and we didn't know how we was gonna wait till we could see Carl and tell him. I remember thinking it was mighty silly for Papa to do all that running when he hadn't done anything wrong.

Mama set there and listened while he told us. She didn't say a word. We never did know whether she knowed it all before, or whether maybe some of it was new to her.

The house Papa had for us in Alexandria was the best one we'd ever lived in, or would ever live in again. There was five rent houses in a row, all alike. A highway run in front of them, and the railroad run behind them. They had four bedrooms, a living room, a real dining room, and a kitchen. Every house had three fireplaces. They had a front porch and a back porch. Had tin roofs. Had outside toilets. Some of them had cold water faucets in the back yard. But the one we moved into had the water faucet in the kitchen. Every bedroom had a closet. And the houses all had electric lights.

Mama sure was proud to have a good place like that. Papa paid $20 a month for it.

We was living in that nice house by the railroad tracks when it came time to harvest sugar cane that fall. The trains carried lots of cane in open cars. They had to slow down before they went through town, and sometimes when they passed our house I'd climb up on a car and throw off a few stalks of cane for us to chew.

We hadn't been living there more than a few months when Papa decided to move us to a farm a few miles out from town. Carl and my cousin John Evans—Uncle Ben's boy—were both in Alexandria with us now, and Papa couldn't get jobs for them at the mill. Generally, he could manage to get a job for one of us. Being the engineer, he had a little influence. But he hadn't been able to do it this time. He was the only one of us working. So he decided to put us out on a farm where we could work.

I'm pretty sure he didn't discuss this with Mama before he decided to move us. Papa was used to being the boss. So the first thing we knowed we was moving. The farm had a little old house on it that was about to fall down. It had a cistern, and we had to draw water in a bucket. That was one time I heard Mama complain. She didn't like that house. She said, "And to think we left that nice house in town for this!"

Papa said, "But the boys will have something to do now." He wanted us to stay busy.

The house had cracks you could throw a cat through, and we couldn't keep warm. But we stayed there until after Christmas. Papa had contracted to have Carl and John make a crop there the next spring, and the man that owned the place had promised to give them some work to do now and then.

Well, he didn't never give them nothing to do that he paid them for. Not only that, he broke the land himself and then wanted the boys to cut sprouts from his drainage ditches to pay him for breaking the land. They had expected to break the land, and they didn't want to cut his sprouts. It was a misunderstanding. Papa was used to the way things was done in Texas, and this man was going by the way they done things there in Louisiana. Papa got mad.

He went and rented another farm close by, where the land hadn't been broke yet. And we was getting ready to move. But this first old farmer said we'd have to pay rent for the two or three months we lived in his house. Papa said he wouldn't pay.

The farmer owned a store that we had to go past to get to the other farm, and he told around that he was going to stop us as we went by. But he didn't. Papa laid off from work the day we moved, and he rode with us on the wagon and carried a rifle. The farmer come out, and when he saw Papa with that gun he just turned around and went back in the store. We was all on the wagon. I was scared.

Mama was a lot prouder when we got to the other farm. The house wasn't anything like as nice as the one we'd had in town, but it was a whole sight better than the one we'd just left.

Carl and John did break the land on this new farm, and they planted the crop. But then they ups and gets jobs in town. Papa had to hire somebody to finish the crop. He put me down there to weigh the cotton when it was picked. And he bought a old T-Model truck so I could haul it to market.

I expect Papa lost money on that deal.

Chapter 11

That fall we went back to Alexandria and moved into another one of them big houses by the railroad.

There was a fair at Alexandria that fall, and Mama's sister, Aunt Martha, came to see us. She had a pretty quilt she entered in the fair and she won first prize.

After we finished with the cotton, Papa put me and the T-Model truck to carrying tie-cutters out to the woods to cut railroad ties. They was men that didn't have no car. They paid me $1.00 apiece a week to carry them out there in the morning and go back and get them in the evening. Gasoline didn't cost but about 12¢ or 15¢ a gallon then.

I also used the truck to haul ash logs to the handle and oar factory there in Alexandria. They made oars for boats and handles for axes. That old truck had a worm drive. Just had a pinion and a worm. Model-T touring cars had a ring drive. But the trucks had a worm drive, they'd pull harder.

While we was living in Alexandria, Papa traded the Maxwell off and got another Model-T touring car. And the first thing he done, he hit a boy on a bicycle. He was used to the Maxwell, where when you wanted to throw the clutch out you pushed the pedal all the way down. He forgot that when you wanted to throw the clutch out in a Model-T you just pushed the pedal halfway down. When he seen that boy on the bicycle in front of him he automatically stepped hard on the clutch and easy on the brake. That didn't work with the Model-T. He had throwed the car into low gear, so he kept right on going. He hit the boy. It didn't hurt him much. Papa took him to the hospital and they said he just had a few scratches. But it tore the bicycle up. Papa bought the boy a new bicycle.

In 1924 Papa left his job at the Long Pine Lumber company there in Alexandria. He wasn't feeling good. He had blacked out on the job a few times. He hadn't hurt himself, or done any damage to the machinery, he had always had enough warning so he could get to a safe place and set down. But it made him irritable. And he begin to have red blotches on his face and hands. The company doctor said he had Bright's disease. He told Papa it was gonna get worse, said there wasn't any cure for it.

Only Alvin and Joe was living with Papa and Mama then. Carl was married, and Curly and me was off working at other sawmills.

Papa sold his Model-T touring car, packed their belongings in his old Model-T truck, and took Mama and the boys and went to his sister Ollie's house near Burke, Texas.

After a few weeks he felt better so he contracted to make a crop on a farm near Burke. He worked outside, cutting sprouts, mending fences, getting the land ready for spring plowing. The red blotches went away. He was feeling a lot better. He said he guessed the doctor was wrong, he wasn't gonna die after all.

Before it was time to lay his crop by that summer he got a job as a engineer at a sawmill in Diboll, working while the regular engineer was on vacation. Then they asked him to work other men's vacation time. He talked me into leaving my job and coming to Burke to finish his crop. If I'd a knowed what I was gonna get into I probably wouldn't a done it.

The man that owned the farm had a old outlaw mule Papa had made the crop with. Papa tried to tell me how to handle that mule. He said, "Every morning when eleven o'clock comes he will think it's dinner time and he will start to the house. What you do is, you just let him go a little ways, then you throw one rein loose and throw the other one around his hip and jerk hard on it and throw him. Then go and get on his head and give him a good whipping." Papa could do that, but not me. I couldn't handle that mule.

[96]

Claude Barr Kennedy standing beside his home, with Fred sitting on the porch. The picture was probably taken in Trinity, around 1926. *Courtesy Effie Kennedy*

The farmer seen I couldn't work that outlaw mule, so he told me, "I've got a real old mule. She'll be all right for you." So I had to plow that old broke-down mule. Papa could get a feller into more scrapes.

Papa worked several men's vacation times in Diboll that summer. The company said they'd like to hire him for a regular hand but they thought he was too old. He was fifty-five.

But a man that knowed him from Groveton come and got him to go and work at a sawmill in New Willard. I guess they didn't think he was too old. He moved the family to New Willard.

In 1926 all of us but Carl was living in Trinity. Papa and Curly and me was working at the sawmill there.

Papa and Mama got to where they was always arguing. It was the first time I'd ever seen them do that. I knowed Papa didn't feel good. By then we knowed that the trouble with him when he left Alexandria was he had got over-het. I knowed that was happening again. I told him, "There's no sense in you killing yourself. I know you don't feel good or you and Mama wouldn't be fussing like this. Curly and me can support the family. I want you to quit that job." So he quit.

He still had the old Model-T truck. He started driving that and doing odd jobs. The superintendent of the mill give him some work to do. He begin to make almost as much as he was making at the mill.

Then a man come from New Willard again and talked him into going back there as engineer at the planing mill. He stayed in New Willard that time six or eight months, about as long as he ever stayed any place.

Sometime in 1928 Papa decided to buy a farm from our good friends Mr. and Mrs. Tryon. The Tryons still lived in Groveton, but they had this farm in the Wesley Chapel community, where Papa and Mama had lived when they was first married, where they was when Papa started running from the law. Mr. Tryon didn't ask no money down. He knowed Papa, and he knowed he was honest. He said we could just pay for the farm along as we got the money.

[98]

Papa thought he wouldn't have no trouble paying for it. He had a plan. He intended to move Mama and the two younger boys and me up there to run the farm, and he planned to keep on working at the mill. He meant to work and pay off the farm and then retire. I think he knowed the time was gonna come when he couldn't stand it to work around them furnaces any longer.

So he moved us up there and told me to take charge of things. But it didn't take long for me to get enough of that. Them younger brothers of mine didn't know nothing about farming. I told Papa, "You come up here and teach Alvin and Joe to farm. I'm gonna go get me a job somewhere and give you my money." And I left.

They stayed on the farm two years. I sent them all the money I could. Papa worked at a little sawmill near there some, and he went to Crockett and laid brick for a while.

I don't know how he knowed how to lay brick. Learned himself I reckon. He'd laid a lots of brick in furnaces but he hadn't never laid none on union jobs. And the union men there in Crockett, they worked against him because he didn't belong to the union. He made good money, all right. But they made it hard on him. He didn't stay too long.

Papa didn't prosper on that farm. It took all he could scrape up just to live, and it wasn't a good living at that. He didn't have nothing left to pay on the farm.

By 1929 times was getting hard in East Texas. Times got hard here before the Depression started in the rest of the country. The big lumbermills had done cut nearly all the pine timber around here, and they were moving out. Lots of people were out of work. Jobs was hard to find. The Trinity County Lumber Company at Groveton was still operating but it wasn't running full time.

Papa lost the farm. He found out another man wanted to buy it and that he could pay Mr. Tryon cash for it. Papa hadn't been able to pay hardly anything on it. And him and Mr. Tryon was friends, so he didn't want to keep him from getting cash for the place. He told Mr. Tryon to sell it to the other man.

He took Mama and Alvin and Joe and went back to Groveton. The reason him to go back down there was they needed him for a certain job. They had to make a graph of how much horsepower the engines pulled. The instrument that made the graph had to be mounted on the driveshaft, and had to be hooked up to electricity. The chief engineer at that time didn't know how to hook it up, so they got Papa down there to do it.

He stayed there a year or so after that, but he wasn't a engineer. He was operating the pump house. The mill wasn't working to full capacity. And it wasn't long till it shut down altogether. But Papa wasn't working there when it shut down. Just before they closed they cut everybody's wages. That made him mad and he quit.

A man couldn't hardly get a job then. Papa went back to the only other kind of work he knowed. He contracted to make a crop on a farm out from Apple Springs. I was out of work then, too, so I helped with the crop. We all worked in the field. Even Mama helped pick cotton. But all we could do was barely make a living.

After we laid our own crop by that year, Papa and me went and worked for another farmer. The man didn't live on his farm, but he had a house there where he kept a cook. Papa and me stayed at the house. We dug his potatoes and gathered his corn and stripped his cane and helped make his syrup—for board and two buckets of syrup a day.

That wasn't anything unusual. People used syrup for money in East Texas. I knowed of one man that paid for his farm by giving the man he bought it from a hundred buckets of syrup a year till he had it paid for. All the general stores would either buy syrup from you, or take it in trade.

The farmer we was working for had another feller working on the farm and living in a sharecropper's house. The owner got the sharecropper to agree, in Papa's presence, that all the syrup would be stored in the regular farmhouse until time come to settle up, and he asked Papa to be responsible for it.

The sharecropper's brother come along and stirred up trouble. He thought the farmer was trying to cheat. He said all the syrup should be stored in the sharecropper's house. Said him and his brother was gonnna keep it in the sharecropper's house.

Well, Papa had been left in charge, and had been told to store that syrup in the farmhouse. And he didn't think that man's brother had any business butting in. He asked him, "Just who are you?"

The feller said, "I ain't got no name."

Papa reached and got a ax handle and said, "Well, I'm gonna name you."

They stored the syrup in the farmhouse.

That farmer we was working for knowed Uncle Amzy. He had made his acquaintance when Amzy was working on a farm in that community after he got out of prison. He told us a little story about him. Said the old farmer Amzy was working for was kinda hard to please, and he kept jawing at Amzy about the way he done the work. One day Amzy just hauled off and give the old man a thrashing. Then he went to the house and told the man's wife, "I guess I'd better leave."

She told him, "No. I don't want you to leave. You just go ahead with your work. The old man will get over it."

So Amzy didn't leave—at least not then. The man that was telling us about it didn't know where Amzy went when he did leave. He hadn't heard anything about him going to Indian Territory.

When we'd gathered our own crop, and it come time to settle up with the man we was renting from Papa told me, said, "You go and settle up with the man."

I said, "But why?"

Papa said, "I'd rather you done it. I'm so bad to lose my temper."

That fall, Mama got sick. Papa got a doctor to come see her. He said she'd have to go to Lufkin to the hospital. They said she had gallstones and they'd have to take them out. When they operated they found she was eat up with cancer. They just sewed her back up. She didn't live but a little while.

Papa and Alvin and Joe kept on living on the rented farm, but I went and got me a job at a little sawmill out from Groveton.

It didn't run only part of the time, so it wasn't much of a job. But I knowed I was lucky to have a job at all. That was where I was working when I met and married a girl named Effie Riordan.

I worked at my little part-time job at the sawmill, and Effie and me lived with Mr. and Mrs. Tryon in Groveton.

One Saturday Mr. Tryon and me was talking with a bunch of men in front of the general store there in Groveton. We were talking about old times around the mill, and they got to talking about Papa, and what a good workman he was, and what a good fist fighter. One of them said, "Remember the time that young feller whipped him in that fight?" They all remembered. Two or three of them said they'd lost money on that fight.

I didn't know about the fight when it happened, but I'd heard off and on over the years that Papa had lost a fight, and I figured out it happened just before we left Groveton that time. I thought I knowed what them men was talking about. But I had a surprise coming.

One of them said, "Remember what old Claude done after he got beat?" They did. They said he went and made himself some wooden knuckles out of pieces of board, and went back and tried to get the young feller to fight him again. They all laughed. They thought it was funny. They didn't know I'd never heard about Papa and them wooden knuckles.

I knowed now why we left town in such a hurry the day after the fight. And I figured I knowed why Papa stopped talking to us about fist fighting.

Effie owned a farm up in Houston County, about thirty miles north of Groveton, that she had inherited from her mother, and she kept wanting her and me to go up there and live. It hadn't had anybody on it for a few years. When I seen how run-down it was—what bad shape the fences was in, how the sprouts had growed up in all the fields, and how the log house needed a new roof—my heart sunk. I didn't see how we'd ever get that place fixed up. But Effie didn't want to live nowhere else, so we moved in and went to work.

Papa was having a hard time making a living for him and the two younger boys. There wasn't any way to get hold of money.

Even if you could raise something to sell, you couldn't get anything for it. Nobody had any money.

When Joe graduated from high school (there were eleven grades in East Texas then) he joined the Tree Army. It was really the Civilian Conservation Corps but folks around here called it the Tree Army. Lots of boys was joining it then, to keep their parents from having to feed them. The government was just making work for the boys. They had them building roads and camping places in the national forests. The government furnished their clothes and their room and board and paid them $15 a month, and sent another $15 to their parents.

We was awful proud of Joe. He was the brightest one in our family. He was the onliest one that graduated from high school.

He hadn't been with the Tree Army but a little over a year when we got word he had died. They said he had pneumonia. It liked to a killed all of us. But Papa took it the hardest.

In 1936 Papa and Alvin come to live with Effie and me. Papa was sixty-seven years old, and he was drawing a old age pension from the state—$30 a month—but he could still do a lots of work. From then on for a long time he done almost all of my plowing.

Some of our neighbors found out Papa was getting a old age pension of $30 a month, and they complained. They said he hadn't ought to be getting that much. Some of them was only getting $11 a month. They got Papa's pension cut back to $11.

By 1940 Effie and me had four children. Dorthy was the oldest. Then come Lydia Jo, Bessie Mae, and Clarence. And we had Papa and Alvin there. I seen I couldn't make a living for all them people on that farm, so I left the farming to Papa and Effie and I went and got me a job at a little sawmill called the Lone Star, between Kennard and Ratcliff.

The mill was getting ready to put in some new boilers. They asked me did I know anybody could do that. I said, "Yes. My daddy can. Him and me together can. He knows everything about boilers and furnaces. He can't handle them heavy wrenches anymore, but he can do the bossing and I can do the work." So that is what we done. We put them boilers in.

When Papa was in his 80s he was still plowing for me. By

that time I had left the Lone Star Mill and was working for the National Forest Service. Ever since 1935 the government had been buying up land around East Texas, anything anybody wanted to sell, and turning it into national forests. They had bought up a lot of land in Houston County, some of it right close to our farm. So I got me a job working for the United States government. Papa worked in the field every day when the ground was ready to break and the crops ready to plant and tend. We farmed thirty-seven acres.

Finally my son Clarence got old enough to take over the plowing. Papa had had a stroke, so he wasn't able to work in the field anymore. I thought he'd be out there, though, bossing Clarence every day. But he wasn't. He never did try to interfere with Clarence and the fieldwork. That surprised me. He always bossed me. I guess he just give it up after he had that stroke.

He mostly just set around the house, and followed Effie around, the rest of the time he lived.

PART III

These short last chapters consist of reminiscences of Effie Riordan Kennedy, Fred's wife, and eight of their children—the family with whom Mr. Claude spent the last years of his life. (Fred's and Effie's four youngest children are not represented here. Erma Jane, born 1947, Mary Jane, born 1949, and Joseph Wilson, born 1950, do not feel they have anything significant to contribute to the story. And Freddy, born 1955, is not mentally capable of contributing.)

Chapter 12
Dorthy (born 1932)

I was my parents' first child.

My grandfather Kennedy and his son Alvin came to live with us in 1936, when I was four years old. I didn't know them well at the time, but they both became important in my life.

My grandfather did not want to be called Grandpa. He taught me to call him Papa. The name stuck and he was Papa from then on, to all of us. He soon earned my respect and my love. He lived with us until he died in 1963, at age ninety-four.

Uncle Alvin always helped me with my schoolwork, a thing he did for my brothers and sisters also. He still lives with my family.

Papa worked in the field all day—plowing, doing whatever there was to be done on our farm. But he always found time to pay a lot of attention to us children. As the years passed he became very special to me. I depended on him. If I'd get discouraged about something he would say, "Just do the best you can. That's all you need to worry about—just do your best." And if he needed to chastise me, he did it in such a way that it didn't make me angry or resentful, it made me feel he loved me enough to correct me.

He never simply said *no* to me, he always gave me a reason for saying it. Sometimes, instead of answering me directly he would tell me to go to a certain place in the Bible and read what it said on the subject. "Read that and see what you think." He never made me feel as if I'd asked something I shouldn't have. When I asked him where babies come from he said, "Where do

you think they come from? God made you. Go read Genesis."
He never lied to us.

And he taught us to be responsible. He'd say, "Always keep
your word. If you tell somebody you're gonna do a thing, you do
it. But if you can't do it, go and apologize and say why you can't
do it."

I really believe Papa lived to the best of his ability the way
he believed. He taught me to be a Christian, and I joined the
Church of Christ. I was the only one in our family who joined his
church.

Papa would be serious when he needed to be. But he was a
great one for poking fun at people. He'd try to get under your
skin. He used to tease me about a little redheaded boy I went to
school with, until I'd get so mad I'd go and bang him on his knee
with my lunch bucket.

In a family as big as ours there was always a lot of work to be
done. And Papa helped with just about everything. He helped
with the 1,300 cans of food we put up every year, with the
twelve hogs we butchered and processed, with the bushels of
yams we stored in tepees in the garden. He almost always did
the churning. He'd say, "Dorthy, come and get the milk ready so
I can churn." We churned almost every day. We ate a lot of butter and Mama liked to keep it fresh.

Sometimes I'd have to take the clothes to the creek and do
the laundry. Mama has an automatic washer and dryer now. But
when I was growing up we washed our clothes down by the
creek. After my sister Bessie got old enough she helped. We
hitched a horse or mule to a slide [sled] and used that to carry
the clothes down there and back. If Papa was around at the time
he'd help with that.

We boiled the clothes in a big iron pot and washed them on
a rub board in a galvanized tub, with homemade lye soap. We
brought the clean clothes back to the house and hung them on
clotheslines and on the yard fence.

Lots of times on summer evenings Papa would be sitting on
the front porch singing, and I'd be in the kitchen helping clean
up after supper. I'd hurry, so I could get out there and sit with

him. Nothing could be as good as sitting on that porch, in the cool, singing gospel songs with Papa, or hearing him talk about the olden days.

Being the oldest child, I had a good bit of responsibility. When I was in high school it was my job to get up early every morning and get breakfast started and get Daddy's and Alvin's lunches packed (they were working at sawmills then) and call Mama and Daddy before I went to the barn to milk. Papa would always get up and get a good fire going for me in the wood cookstove. I didn't have much time because I had to catch the school bus at seven o'clock. Papa was a big help.

Papa went to town with Daddy every Saturday, and he'd bring home peppermint candy. It was always peppermint, no other kind. There wouldn't be a lot of it, Papa didn't have much money. All of us could have some candy, but my brother Buddy [Clarence] generally got most of it. Buddy was the first boy in the family, and he was spoiled. Papa would pout if Mama spanked Buddy—he'd stay mad all day.

Papa bought our first radio. But he allowed us to listen only when he felt it was proper. We could hear the Grand Ole Opry on Saturday nights. And we could listen to the news. That was all.

Papa was real bad to argue with people about religion. He had read the Bible through several times, and he just about knew it by heart. He thought he knew what it meant, and he thought his interpretation was the only right one. He and my other grandfather used to argue about it a lot when Grandpa Riordan would be visiting us.

Papa would start the argument with something like: "I belive you are an infidel," or "You can't find any place in the Bible where it says anything about a Baptist Church. It only talks about the Church of Christ."

They'd be going at it in the kitchen, maybe, and Mama would finally say, "Why don't you two go out on the porch and be quiet?" Sometimes Grandpa Riordan would get so mad he wouldn't talk to Papa. But Papa wouldn't give it up. If Grandpa tried to take a nap, Papa would follow him back to the bedroom and try to continue the argument.

And once Papa said to me. "Your Grandpa Riordan would argue with *anything*. I saw him out there awhile ago arguing with a fence post." This was said in Grandpa Riordan's hearing, and calculated to get a rise out of him.

Once in a while Papa and Daddy would have a little disagreement, generally because Daddy would get tired of Papa's trying to boss him. Papa would get angry and declare he intended to leave and go live with his son Carl in Lufkin. Daddy would say, "Well, all right. Go ahead if you want to." But Mama never said that. She didn't want to hurt Papa's feelings.

And one time Papa actually did leave. He left on the school bus, along with us children, and then he caught the regular bus from Kennard to Lufkin. When we were all standing there by the road, waiting for the school bus, I looked over and saw Papa wiping his eyes. He was crying. I felt so bad I could hardly stand it. We begged him to go back to the house but he wouldn't. He went on and stayed with Uncle Carl for a few days. Then he came back. Everybody, including Papa, just acted like he hadn't been away.

Papa worked one winter as a kind of watchman for a small sawmill that kept moving from place to place in our community. He had a little trailer of a thing he lived in, and he did his own cooking. I have some of the utensils he used then: a fork, a spoon, and a case knife. And I have his cast-iron frying pan—I still make my corn bread in it.

After I was grown and out on my own, Papa would be tickled to death to see me when I'd go home. And that would make me feel so good. His eyes would light up and he'd say, "Hello, Dorthy! When did you get here?"

I miss Papa. I could always go and talk to him about my problems. He seemed to know how my heart felt.

Chapter 13
Lydia Jo (born 1935)

When I was little I remember Papa had a couple of big old logging mules he was trying to work our farm with. He had trouble with them. They ran away with him once, and dragged him a little ways and skinned him up some. But he was determined to keep on using those mules. Daddy said Papa was stubborn in his ways.

When I look back on it, it seems to me that Papa was trying to prove to himself and everybody else that he wasn't getting old. I remember that he used to jump a wide ditch along the side of the road when he went to the mailbox. He could have walked a little farther and crossed without jumping.

We had lots of babies at our house, and Papa was always helping Mama take care of them when he wasn't working in the field. He was awfully good to all of us, and we loved him very much. But he teased us a lot. When he'd tease me until I couldn't bear it any more, I'd go and stand on his feet, facing him, and stomp up and down as hard as I could. That must have been comical, because I was always short and he was such a big tall man.

The winter he worked as a caretaker for that portable sawmill in the woods around Kennard, he did his own cooking. Daddy went to see about him often, and Mama would send food. Daddy generally carried some of us children when he went. I remember tasting some corn bread and butterbeans Papa had cooked and thinking, "Poor Papa—he doesn't know how to cook." We children worried about him. We told Daddy we wanted Papa to come back and live with us.

Mules used for logging had to be bigger and stronger than those generally used for farming. These mules are the kind Mr. Claude tried to farm with. *Courtesy Temple-Eastex, Inc.*

The only thing I ever saw Papa read was the Bible. He read it a lot. He said he had read it from cover to cover many times. He was always quoting from it. And when he did, he could tell you exactly what chapter and verse it came from. He loved to discuss the Bible with anybody he could get to talk about it. It sounded to me like arguing, but he called it debating.

Sometimes the Baptist preacher would come to our house for Sunday dinner. Mama and Daddy would be apprehensive at such times because they'd be afraid Papa would get into an argument with him. And Papa always did, in spite of Mama's telling him ahead of time not to.

It seemed like Papa was always itching for an argument about religion. People who knew him generally tried to stay away from that subject, but he'd pick at them until they'd finally get into it. He would sometimes say, "You have to belong to the Church of Christ if you want to go to heaven." And I have heard him, when he'd be mad at whoever he was arguing with, say, "You can either believe like the Church of Christ people, or you can go to hell—just suit yourself."

There wasn't a Church of Christ near us, so Papa would go with us to the Ivie Baptist Church. Daddy said he behaved himself fairly well then.

And he always went to funerals, no matter what church they were held at. Even when he didn't know the person who had died, he went. When we asked him why, he said, "I want people to come to my funeral."

Our Sunday School teacher at Ivie Church expected us to respond with a Bible verse instead of *here* when she called the roll. We had to give the verse and say where in the Bible it appeared. When I hadn't had time to memorize a new verse I'd fall back on "Jesus wept." Papa used to say it a lot. He said it was the shortest verse in the Bible. I still remember where it's found: Saint John, eleventh chapter, thirty-fifth verse.

Papa bought peppermint candy and other little things for us children—as much as he could afford on his $11-a-month pension. Once he bought a radio. He said it was for us, but he kept it in his room, on a shelf above his bed. And he wouldn't let us turn it on very often because it ran on batteries. He had a wooden box beside his bed, where he kept some of his personal things. I used to sneak in there and climb on that box so I could reach the radio, and turn it on and listen to music.

Papa lived to be ninety-four and the last year or so of his life he became just like a child. Mama would have to make him do what she thought he ought to do. I know she had her hands full with him. But she kept him at home and took care of him until he died. It was what she wanted to do.

Chapter 14

Bessie Mae (born 1936)

I was the third of twelve children. Papa came to live with us
when I was a baby. He was already past sixty-five, but he was
healthy. He worked on our farm all of the time I was growing up.

When he wasn't working in the field he played with us children a lot. He spent all of his little bit of money on us. Well, he
spent it mostly on my brother Buddy, who was two years younger
than me. He bought Buddy a little red wagon, and later he
bought Buddy a bicycle. Mama said those things were for all of
us, that we could all play with them—and we did. But everybody knew Papa got them for Buddy. Papa loved us all, but he
favored Buddy. Buddy would cry until Papa would persuade
Mama to let him go to Kennard with him and Daddy every Saturday. None of us girls ever got to go—we had to stay home and
work.

We had an old dog named Queenie, and she died. Papa put
her in Buddy's wagon and took her off down in the woods. We all
followed along, crying, and he tried to comfort us. He didn't
bury the dog—he just dumped it down there. We kids would
walk down there every once in a while and look at it, and we'd
cry. We even went down there and cried over it when there
wasn't anything but bones.

Papa was a big tease. He loved to hoo-rah us kids. One time
I got lost while I was trying to find one of our cows that had gotten out of the pasture. I wound up way over there halfway to

Kennard. An old bachelor who lived in that area found me and brought me home. I was just a little kid, maybe ten years old. But Papa hoo-rahed me about that. He said the old man was my boyfriend. He'd tell me, "I saw your boyfriend when I was in Kennard today. He'll be out here after while to see you." I never could take hoo-rahing. I'd squall, and boohoo, and stomp.

Papa would go to the Ivie Baptist Church with us, off and on, because there wasn't a Chruch of Christ near us. I remember that once he went to Ivie for a long time. I think he even taught a Sunday School class for a while. But one Sunday somebody refused to let him take communion because he wasn't a Baptist. That made him mad, so he quit going to church there.

Mama's sister Nancy used to come to visit us. We children all liked her a lot, and we'd hang onto her and pay a lot of attention to her. She always played with us, took us to pick blackberries and things like that.

Aunt Nancy belonged to the Pentecostal Church, and she knew the Bible quite well. She and Papa could get into some really big arguments. Sooner or later Papa would get around to saying that anybody who didn't belong to the Church of Christ was going to hell. Aunt Nancy would get mad and go home. I always thought this was Papa's way of getting rid of her. I think he was jealous because we were paying her too much attention.

Papa sang bass. And I wanted to sing with him, so I'd try to sing bass. I thought that was the right way because that was how he sang. When I got older I found out I had a high soprano voice.

Papa was in his middle 80's when I graduated from high school and went away from home. He was active for several more years. He helped my parents raise my younger brothers and sisters, just as he had helped them raise us older ones.

Chapter 15
Clarence Edward (born 1938)

My name is Clarence, but everybody in my family calls me Buddy.

Papa was already living at our house when I was born and he was still living there when I left home in 1956. He was a natural part of my family.

For several years I was the only boy among three older and two younger sisters. People said Papa was partial to me. I didn't notice it. But it might have been true. I don't think he really spoiled me very much. For one thing, Mama wouldn't allow it. If Papa bought something for me she said it belonged to my sisters, too, and we all had to share it. The only thing I remember his buying that I didn't have to share was a little change purse. He had one and I was always wanting to play with it, so he bought one for me. It was all mine. But it didn't do me much good. I soon lost it.

Until I started to school I was with Papa constantly. I tagged along behind him when he plowed in the field. I sat beside him, often on his lap, when he smoked his pipe on the front porch. I went with him to town on Saturdays.

Every Saturday Daddy would take our old Model-A Ford coupe that had a little wooden truck bed built on the back, and go to Kennard to get his paycheck cashed, and to buy groceries and whatever we needed. Papa always went along. And I tried my best to get to go also.

Sometimes Mama would say I couldn't go because I hadn't

finished my chores. We always had chores, everybody had to work. I couldn't stand for Daddy and Papa to go to town without me, so I'd cry. Then Papa would say, "Effie, why don't you let the boy go? I'll help him do whatever it is you have for him to do when we get back." And Mama would generally give in—she had to get really angry before she'd cross Papa. She'd do it sometimes, though.

There was what was called a spit-and-whittle bench in front of Mr. Ab Westerman's general store in Kennard, and Papa would head straight for that. There'd be other men already there. All day long that bench would be full of men. Some would wander off and others drift in. It was a place to visit with neighbors, to swap big tales, complain about the government, argue over the Bible. It was a way for Papa to keep in touch with society.

Daddy would be off attending to his own affairs, but I'd stick close to Papa. If I pestered him he would buy me an ice-cream cone to keep me quiet.

A lot of what the men talked about had to do with things that had happened in their lives. Something would cause one of them to remember an important incident, and his telling about it would set off a string of remembrances by other men. I heard lots of these tales over and over, and sometimes I thought they got bigger with each telling.

The men talked about hard times, and good times, about war, and about their ailments. And they talked a lot about politics.

They were generally in agreement when they talked about the way the national government was being run—mostly they didn't like it. But they split right down the middle when the discussion changed to local politics. They were all Democrats, and the local officeholders were Democrats—we didn't have Republicans here then. The state and local officials had their friends and followers who staunchly, and noisily, defended their every act. But they also had their detractors. And those Democrats could be real outspoken against a Democrat they didn't agree with. Being a one-party electorate didn't keep down the argument. Sometimes it got pretty hot.

And they talked a lot about religion. That's what Papa liked to talk about better than anything. Well, what he mostly wanted to do was express his own opinion, convince other people they were wrong and he was right. He'd quote from the Bible to prove a point, whether it had anything to do with religion or not.

People didn't do much arguing with Papa about religion or the Bible. For one thing, he was a lot older than most of the others, and I think they kind of respected his age. Also, he had read the Bible through a lot of times, and he knew it by heart, just about. I never did hear anybody win an argument with him when they were talking about the Bible.

But one Saturday there was a middle-aged preacher there who seemed to feel real important. He made a statement about the Bible, and Papa told him he was wrong. The man got mad, and then Papa got mad. Papa was in his 80s at the time but he was cocky. He rolled up his sleeves and told the preacher, "Take off your glasses and I'll learn you a few things."

They were about to get into it when Daddy came and said it was time to go home. Daddy would generally let us stay around there until Papa was ready to leave, even if that was the middle of the afternoon. But I suppose he decided he'd better stop things before they got rough that day.

Papa pointed his finger at the preacher and said "Go home and read your Bible and get a little smarter."

The preacher shook his fist at Papa.

Daddy pushed us into the car and we took off.

I believe one of the reasons Papa could win so many arguments was that he could generally tell what other people were thinking. He seemed to keep a little bit ahead of them.

When I was maybe four or five Papa bought me a little wagon. He'd pull me around in the yard and up and down the dirt road in front of our house. And once when his sisters came to visit, and I started crying because I thought I wasn't getting enough attention, he put me in the wagon and pulled me down the road to the creek. Mama got all over him about that. She thought he should have been talking with his sisters. I remember she made me go in the back yard and leave Papa alone.

[118]

That little wagon was a nice toy. But by the time it got divided up among five or six of us nobody got to play with it a lot.

And once Papa bought a bicycle. He caught a ride to Crockett and bought it, and he rode it home. Crockett was about twenty-five miles from our house, and Daddy hardly ever went there. The bicycle was secondhand. I don't know how much he paid for it, but it couldn't have been much—all he had was his little old-age pension check. My sisters felt hurt because Papa bought the bicycle for me. But it didn't seem that it was just for me—Mama said we all had to share it.

Papa sometimes talked to me about things that had happened in his life. My grandmother died before I was born, but I got the impression that Papa loved her very much, and that he never got over missing her. Some things, he talked about a lot. He'd tell the same stories over and over, especially after he got older. His eyes would get soft when he'd tell about the happy times they'd had, when they had their first home in Groveton, when they sat on the front steps and sang gospel songs. Sometimes he'd cry a little when he talked of their children that died, or about when Grandmother herself died. But when he talked about the time he was accused of stealing lumber, or when his boss said he had ruined a piece of pipe, he'd look like he was ready to fight.

Some people might have found Papa annoying at times, but I don't think anybody ever found him uninteresting.

He was an important person in my life.

Chapter 16

Barbara Lou Ella (born 1940)

I was the fifth of twelve children. I never thought of our family without Papa. He was there all the time I was growing up.

He teased all of us. He always picked at me a lot. When Mama would cut my hair he'd say, "Looks like she turned a bowl over your head and cut around it," and he'd keep saying, "Chippie, get your hair cut, hair cut, hair cut, short like mine."

At the table, if we'd ask him to pass the bread, he'd say, "Oh, eat your dinner and leave the bread alone." Then he'd grin and pass the bread.

If he'd hear me whistling he'd say, "A whistling girl and a crowing hen always comes to no good end."

He always said the blessing over the food. Nobody asked him to. He just took it for granted that was his privilege. And most of the time, after he'd finish saying the blessing he'd say, "Now, back your ears and all dive in." Once in a while he'd forget and say that ending when we'd have company, and Mama would be embarrassed.

Papa teased me, and I teased him. Sometimes when he'd be taking a nap I'd peck on his head with my finger and he'd think it was a bird. Or I thought he did. And sometimes I'd pull his toe when he was asleep. I wanted him to get up and play with me. He'd jump up and chase me. I loved that.

When he got older and couldn't take care of himself very well, I was the one who washed his hair and cut his toenails. Sometimes the nails would be real hard, and maybe I'd get them cut a little too close, and he'd grin and rub his knuckles on my head, hard, to try to even the score.

We all ran to Papa for sympathy when Mama spanked us. We'd crawl up in his lap and he would rock us and feel sorry for us.

Chapter 17
Eva Dell (born 1942)

I came along in the middle of our family. I had four sisters and one brother older than me.

My first memories of Papa are that he brought us peppermint candy when he went to town. And that all of us children got lots of attention from him. We could sit in his lap and he would rock us and sing to us. Sometimes he told us things about when he was a child. He said he had a twin brother that died when he was a baby. I always thought that was important—that Papa was a twin.

Daddy worked away from home—at sawmills, and later for the United States Forest Service. Papa did our farming. Mama helped in the field a lot. She also raised big gardens. And all of us children had to help with the work.

Dorthy was the oldest child. She had a lot of responsibility. When she wasn't in school she had to manage the house and do the cooking and take care of the babies. Bessie and Lydia helped. And Dorthy used to bribe us younger kids to get us to help— like dust the furniture, or clean the chewing gum off the floor when she was getting ready to mop. She'd bake us cookies, or maybe give us a cup of coffee with sugar in it. After she graduated from high school and left home Bessie took over the cooking, and Lydia kept the house. Later, Barbara did the cooking. Chores kept being passed down as the older ones graduated and left.

If Papa wasn't working in the field he'd look around and see what we were doing, and he'd come and help. We never asked

Mr. Claude with some of his grandchildren, 1953. *Foreground:* Claud; *front row, from left:* Mary Jane, Erma Jane, Mr. Claude holding Joseph Wilson, Clara Bell; *back row, from left:* Eva Dell, Bessie Mae, and Barbara Lou Ella. *Courtesy Effie Kennedy*

him to help, but he did. When I was little, one of my chores was to carry in the stovewood. He used to come and help me, after he'd worked in the field all day.

And when I was fourteen and had to take over the splitting of the wood—because my brother Buddy had graduated from high school and gone from home, and my brother Claud had

[123]

asthma—Papa taught me how to handle the ax, and how to hit the wood to make it split. Nobody had had time to show me how to do that, so I was out there wearing myself out trying to get that wood split. Papa said, "You're hitting it too many times. You have to learn to hit it at the right angle." And he'd hit it once and it'd split wide open.

Papa always used good English. Well, he'd have little sayings he'd say a lot—like "really?" or "I do declare." But that's just sayings, that's not bad English. He'd say "I swear!" Just like he couldn't believe something.

Alvin used good English, too. He always helped us with our lessons. I couldn't read very fast. And after I'd do my chores at night I'd be real tired, and reading would put me to sleep. Alvin could read fast, so he would read whatever I was supposed to read, and he'd write it down. He'd maybe make five pages. I'd read that and make two pages out of it. That's the way I got my book reports.

When I was in high school, one of my jobs was to clean Papa's room, and make his bed up fresh, and see that he put on clean clothes. He dipped snuff then, and he was getting messy with it. He'd miss his spit can and spit on his shirt, or on his sheets, or against the wall. He was getting cataracts on his eyes and couldn't see very well. He didn't like to be changing clothes all the time. I guess he thought it was too much trouble—he wore long heavy union suits winter and summer. Sometimes I had quite a time with him. But I never resented him. I was part of the family. He was part of the family.

One thing that stands out in my memory of Papa is that he stayed strong and active into his nineties. Other old people seemed like they tended to get lazy. He never did.

Chapter 18

Claud (born 1944)

I was the seventh child in our family. Papa was 75 years old when I was born. He had been living with my folks for several years already, and he was with us all the time I was growing up. I was named for him, but I don't spell my name exactly as he spelled his—I don't use that last "e."

When I was little we had a big cast-iron wood heater in the living room. About four o'clock every winter morning Papa would get up and fire up that old heater with pine knots. Its roaring would wake me up and I'd come out there and stand by it. Sometimes it would be red hot. We kept a big pan of water on it, so the older children could wash up before they went to school.

Papa would put me on his lap by the stove. That is where he taught me to tie my shoes, tying the bows together in a single knot so they would not come loose.

I followed him around, especially before I was old enough to go to school. He used to loan me his pocketknife to whittle with. He taught me how to use it, and to respect it as a dangerous tool. Papa taught me many things like that.

Papa dipped Sweet Garrett snuff. In the summer he sat on the porch a lot. He would pull his rocking chair to the shady west end in the mornings, then drag it to the east end in the evenings, and he'd spit out into the yard. He could spit through two fingers and hit a cat in the eye at fifty paces.

On Saturdays Papa went to Kennard to the barbershop to get shaved. I think he had shaved himself when he first came to live with us, but when he got old he went to the barbershop once a week. I heard Neal Butler, the barber, say that Papa had the toughest beard he ever saw.

Papa was the main attraction at the barbershop, where a lot of men gathered to talk and visit as well as to get haircuts and shaves. He had a special kind of humor, and hardly anybody escaped it. He would look up and see somebody coming in the door, maybe, and he'd say to the barber, "Well, if it ain't the old unforgettable what's his name! Last time I saw him he was riding a bicycle, now he's driving a Cadillac."

Or, he might say, "Hey! That's that man I was telling you about awhile ago—the one that rides the bicycle backwards."

Or, to a man who was accompanied by his wife: "Where's that other woman you was with the other day?"

Or, to a friend or neighbor: "Where you been? I've been trying to get a line on you, but all I could get was a fishing line. Wasn't nothing on it so I throwed it back in."

Papa and his humor was big talk amongst my schoolmates who saw him around Kennard. He was well-liked by everybody there.

He never went to Kennard without buying a little sack of peppermint candy sticks to take home to us children. When I went with him he'd buy me an ice-cream cone.

Papa liked to argue about the Bible, especially with preachers. He always managed to have the last comment. Well, he generally had the last word no matter who he was arguing with, or what it was about. One time one of our neighbors wanted him to help catch a cow that had gotten into our pasture. Papa was plowing and he didn't want to stop. He told the man, "It's your cow. Go chase her yourself." The man got mad. Papa told him, "Go stick your tail in the creek and cool off."

Sometimes Papa told me tales. One that he told a lot used to make my heart about jump out my mouth. He said one time he was walking through the woods at night, going to read the Bible to somebody who was blind. It was real dark and he wasn't carrying a light. Said he wasn't having any trouble finding his

Mr. Claude, age 87, in front of the Fred Kennedy home, 1956. *Courtesy Effie Kennedy*

way, though—he was following along a path he'd traveled lots of times.

He said he was walking along there and he got to wondering what it would be like to be blind. He decided it would be dark like tonight, all the time. Said he got to thinking about being

[127]

blind and wasn't paying much attention to anything else. Suddenly he heard a rustling in the leaves, off to the side of the path. He thought it was probably a deer. Then something came from behind and grabbed his shoulders. He didn't know what it was. It had two hands, or two paws, or something.

He said he twisted and lunged forward and started running. The "thing," whatever it was, didn't follow him. He got to a neighbor's house and told what had happened. They took the neighbor's dogs back and put them on the trail, and they bayed something down in the river bottom. The men could hear a big fight going on. Two dogs were killed, and the ones that came back were all scratched and cut up.

Papa said they never did know what it was that caught him by the shoulders. He always thought it was a bear, but he wasn't sure.

He'd tell that, and I'd be afraid to get down off his lap.

Papa wasn't afraid of anything.

He told me that when he was a boy people used to give him nickels to get him to fight other boys. I think he grew big early. When I knew him he was well over six feet tall. He was slim. And he had long arms. His hands hung down nearly to his knees.

I had great respect for him. Of course we were taught to respect him. But my respect didn't have anything to do with duty—it was real, and natural. I think I was as close to him as I was to my father. Maybe even closer—Daddy was always off at work, and Papa was there around the house.

When he was hoo-rahing and cutting up, he was all silliness and teasing. But he could be very serious, and then it was no nonsense. If we had a problem, we could go and talk to him, and he'd take time to listen.

I don't think the people Papa hoo-rahed held any of it against him. When he was old and sick lots of them came by the house to chat with him.

A lot of people came to his funeral.

Chapter 19
Clara Bell (born 1946)

I was in the tenth grade when Papa died. He had been sick for a year or more, and hadn't been like himself. But I remember him when he was healthy, and I like those memories best.

Of course one of the most outstanding things about Papa was his knowledge of the Bible, and the way he seemed bent on picking an argument with people about it. But my older brothers and sisters have talked about that, so I won't dwell on it. It didn't bother me when I was little, but after I got older I'd be embarrassed when he'd start arguing with our guests.

There wasn't anything Papa couldn't do. And he made us think there wasn't anything we couldn't do, either. He'd find the time to help us kids when we needed somebody. Mama was always busy with other things, and Daddy was always away at work. Papa would take time to show us how to do things, explain how to go about it. If we'd break a doll, for instance, and we'd be crying, Papa would say, "Let's see if we can't fix that." And he'd show us how to do it.

He used to say, "Never say *can't*. You can do what you think you can do." He made me feel that I could do anything I needed to.

And I generally needed to do a lot. Mama had to have us help her with the work, she always had so much to do. All of us were given a lot of responsibility when we were quite young. I think, now, that it was good for us. I believe that is why we can do what we need to now.

[129]

When Mama would be having a baby, Papa would take us kids down in the woods and keep us out of the house. There were two pear trees back there, and that's where we'd go. Papa would play with us. We'd build playhouses out of pine boughs. One of us would be the Mama and one the Daddy, and the littlest ones would be the children. If it would be the time of year for blackberries or huckleberries to be ripe we'd pick them and use them for our playhouse food.

We'd be off like that, and when we'd come back to the house we'd have a new baby.

Papa used to help us make what he called "muskeydine wine." All we did was put a little sugar and a few muscadines in a jar of water. We never let it stay more than two or three days. We couldn't wait. We were in too big a hurry to drink it. We called it wine. We thought it was wine.

Once Papa was chopping stovewood and he hit my little sister Mary Jane in the head with the ax. He was chopping, and some of us were picking up the wood and carrying it in the house. Mary Jane was little. She ran up to get a stick of wood when he already had the ax in the air, and he couldn't quite stop it. It just hit a glancing lick, but it cut her head, and she was bleeding something awful. It liked to scared all of us to death.

Papa picked her up and started for the house, yelling for Mama. They had to send one of the older children to a neighbor's house to get him to come and take her to the doctor— Daddy was at work and we didn't have a car at the house. The doctor took some stitches and Mary Jane got all right.

The last year or two that Papa lived he was always sitting in his rocker on the front porch, when he wasn't in bed. He dipped snuff, and spit out into the yard. He'd miss a lot, and hit the porch. I'd have to clean that snuff spit off the porch. I didn't particularly like that. But I loved Papa.

He'd be sitting there, rocking, and maybe we'd all be busy working or playing, and all of a sudden he'd say, "Peckerwood pecking on a long tall pine. Wants a chaw of bakker but he can't have none of mine." Or maybe he'd say, "Jesus wept. And well he might—the devil's gonna get us Campbellites [a term sometimes applied to members of the Church of Christ]." He'd be trying to have some fun. These little humorous sayings would just come out. I think it meant he wanted us to pay him some attention.

We sometimes pestered him. We'd slip up behind him and peck on his head and try to make him think it was a bird. Or we'd draw a feather across the back of his neck. We thought it was fun. We learned teasing from him. But, especially after he was old, he didn't take teasing too well. He'd threaten to tell Mama on us. But he never did.

He never spanked us. He'd tell us to run if Mama was getting after us. And if she punished us he'd hold us on his lap and console us. Mama claimed he spoiled us.

I was named for Papa's favorite sister, Aunt Clara Bell. They said Papa was always close to her. He didn't live but a short time after Aunt Clara Bell died.

Chapter 20
Effie

Mr. Claude lived with Fred and me for nearly thirty years. Sometimes I wonder how we'd ever raised our family without him—we had so many children, and they come so close together. He done a lot of taking care of them, and the littleuns was always hanging on him. After he got old and sick I used to tell him, "Papa, don't let them wear you out." And sometimes I'd tell them to go on and play and stop bothering him. But he'd wait till I went in the other room and I'd hear him tell them, "Come on, you can set on my lap now."

When one of them would have colic or something and I'd have to be up with it at night I'd try to be real quiet. I didn't want to wake Fred because he'd have to work the next day. But Papa would always hear me, seemed like, and he'd come in there and build up the fire. Then he'd hold the baby while I got it some aspirin or paregoric or something. And he'd stay right there and keep the fire going, and help with the baby till we could get it eased off enough to go back to bed.

For fifteen or twenty years Papa done almost all the plowing and raising of our field crops. I raised the gardens. I didn't allow Fred or Papa to touch that. I's afraid they'd mark a row out crooked, or let the horse step on a hill of beans. I always liked my gardens done just right. But Papa done the work in the field. Well, after the younguns got big enough to work they helped, when they wasn't in school. We never kept them out of school to help with the work, like some people done, like my parents done. Fred and me was determined that ours would all get a education. Didn't neither of us get much schooling, and we wanted our children to be educated. They all finished high school, and most of them went on to some kind of college. Except Freddy, our youngest.

Freddy has always been different. He didn't develop the right way, his body or his mind neither one. He is twenty-eight years old now. I have always kept him at home and taken care of him myself. He can say a few words, and since we've had him fitted with special shoes he can walk pretty good by himself, in the house. He feeds himself, and he can take his own bath if somebody helps him in and out of the tub. He's a important part of our family.

Papa didn't have no whole lot of money, but he spent all he had on our children. He'd buy them little treats when they went to town with him. And when Buddy—Clarence—was three or four Papa bought a little wagon. He'd pull them in that wagon, up and down the road in front of our house. Later on, he bought a bicycle. It was a boy's bicycle but the girls rode it. Buddy was our first boy. Then we had more girls before we had another boy. The girls always claimed Papa and me spoiled them boys. But I don't think I did. I tried to treat them all the same.

When Papa was raising our field crops he liked to plant by the moon. When it was dark-looking and hanging heavy he'd say it was full of rain. If it looked light he'd say, "Well, we can plant now—it ain't gonna rain too much." He used to try to get me to plant my potatoes and onions in the dark of the moon.

He claimed if owls hollered in the morning it was gonna rain, and if they hollered at night it was a sign of dry weather. And when his predictions didn't come true, he'd say, "All signs fail once in occasion."

He taught us how to store sweet potatoes in a tepee in the garden. He'd pile them potatoes up, trying to make the stack as high and narrow as possible. Then he'd cover the top and sides with a foot or so of pine straw [dry pine needles]. He'd stand a wide board up against that, on the north side, letting it stand up maybe a foot or two higher than the stack of potatoes and straw. Then he'd stand another board, a shorter one, up on the south side, and let the top of it come up under the board he'd put on the north side. He'd cover the rest of the stack with boards. Then he'd shovel dirt up against it and over the top, maybe a foot of dirt. When we wanted potatoes we'd go out there and remove a little board next to the south side and pull us out some potatoes. Then we'd cover the place back over real good. Them potatoes would keep all winter.

Papa used to go to the field early in the morning and not come back to the house till noon. And when he came in he always said the exact same thing to me: "Well, you know, I'm getting lazy. I stopped once. About ten o'clock. When I was lighting my pipe." He smoked a pipe most of the time he lived with us. He didn't start dipping snuff till he got old.

We was still living in the old log house my father built, but it was about to fall down. The roof was bad, and there were big cracks between the logs. It was nice and cool in there in the summer, but in the winter we had trouble staying warm. We'd build a big fire in the fireplace, and everybody stand around it, and get hot on one side and cold on the other. So when we got to where we could, we built us a lumber house.

We sealed that house up good and tight. And we bought one of them big old long cast-iron heaters. It had two eyes on top, and you could put a great big log in it. We thought, now, everybody would stay comfortable. But the younguns started having a lot of colds and sickness. The doctor said it was because we was keeping the house too hot. He said we ought to crack a winder a little, even in cold weather.

The house was staying hot, all right. But it wasn't Fred and me doing it—it was Papa. He'd get that house so hot it'd might near catch on fire. Seemed like he stayed cold all the time.

In warm weather Papa liked to set on the front porch and smoke his pipe. And lots of times he'd have one or two of the younguns on his lap. Well, one day he come bringing Buddy to me. I guess Buddy was maybe two or three years old. He was limp, and he had something black all over his face and in his mouth. I grabbed him and wiped his face and mouth with a wet rag, and I run out in the yard with him and put him up on my shoulder. He vomited, real good. He was white as a sheet. But he begin to feel better, and he wanted to go to sleep. I wouldn't let him. I had always heard you shouldn't let one of them go to sleep if it was real sick, so I tried to keep him awake.

I said, "Papa, what on earth was that on this baby's face?"

He kinda hung his head and said, "I think he might a been playing with my pipe—and got the stem unscrewed."

Fred said I got after Papa pretty bad about that. But I don't think I was hard on him. I think I just told him not to let any of them get his pipe again.

He spoiled the younguns in a way. He was too good to them. He couldn't hardly tell them *no*. Once when two of his sisters come to see him, and they's only going to be here for a few hours, Papa let Buddy talk him into taking him for a ride in the little wagon. I didn't know it at first. When I found out about it, there was Papa, pulling that youngun up and down in front of the house. I went out there and said, "Papa, why ain't you in there visiting with Aunt Clara Bell and Aunt Mag?"

He said, "Buddy Boy cried when I tried to put him off."

I said, "Buddy Boy, you get out of that wagon and take it in the backyard, and you stay there!"

That's how Papa was. He couldn't bear to hear one of them cry. It didn't make no difference who was here, if one of the children started to cry he'd take it and go rock it. He'd rock them and sing to them, and he'd have them asleep in no time. He done them all that way.

Papa had a stroke seven years before he died, and he set on the porch a lot after that. He didn't go back to the field anymore. But he didn't take any waiting on. He was awful independent. He waited on himself. And he expected everybody else to do the same. he couldn't hardly stand it for some of the rest of them to ask me to bring them a glass of water or something. He'd say, "I never in my life asked nobody to bring me a glass of water."

The stroke didn't leave him too awful bad off. He'd help the children with their chores some. And when they was all in school he'd foller me around a lot when I'd be cooking or working around the house. And seemed like he'd want to talk about things that happened a long time ago.

[135]

Mr. Claude on the steps of the Fred Kennedy home, where he lived for almost thirty years. *From left:* Fred Wallace Kennedy, Joseph Wilson Kennedy, Freddie Kennedy, and Claude Barr Kennedy holding Clarence's daughter Pamela. *Courtesy Clarence Kennedy*

He told about his Grandpa Phillips, his mother's father. He said he only saw him once. Said the old man come to see them, and he had a man with him that had been his slave, and that still worked for him. Said his grandpa was a setting up there, real straight, in that buggy, and this colored man was setting there beside him, driving the team. When they got to the house the man got down and went and helped his grandpa down, making a big to-do about it. Papa said he had never seen anything like that, and he thought he was gonna have to laugh right in their faces. Said they stayed three or four days. And every day the old man and his servant would go hunting, or fishing. And one day he had the servant write a letter for him. And every night the man would shine the old man's shoes. When they got ready to leave his grandpa give each of the children a penny, and give their mama a silver dollar.

He talked about drying beef. Said when they lived in Anderson County, after his father died, some of their relatives dried beef. They'd take ropes and pull it up high in a tree, way up there. Said seemed like flies didn't bother it if you kept it up high. They'd pull up a whole quarter, and it'd get a dry crust all over it. Must a been in the wintertime. When they wanted some they'd let it down and cut off whatever they needed, then they'd pull the quarter back up in the tree.

He said his mother used to send him out to dig toothbrushes. I knowed what he was talking about. My mother dug her own toothbrushes. They used a little weed, or shrub. Seems like they called it beggar roots. You could pull it up and it'd have little roots, and you could chew the roots and make toothbrushes. You could dip them brushes in sody and brush your teeth. But what people used them mostly for was to dip snuff. They'd take the brush end and stick it in the snuff box and get some snuff on it, then stick it back between their jaw teeth and their cheek and let the other end stick out. Mostly they used snuff like that right after a meal. My mother did. She'd go out on the porch and set on the step and use that toothbrush and snuff for about ten minutes, then she'd get up and go wash her mouth out, put the brush up, and wash up her dishes and do whatever else she had to do. She didn't use no more snuff till she eat again. But some people used it all during the day, just like people smoke.

Papa dipped snuff after he stopped smoking his pipe. But he didn't use a brush. He'd just pull his lower lip out and dump half a teaspoon or so of snuff between his gums and his lip. He had a little tin box he carried his snuff in. You could buy them little boxes for a nickel, with snuff in them. They'd hold enough snuff for a day or two. Papa used Levi Garrett snuff. It come in a dark brown bottle with a cork stopper. He'd fill his little box from the bottle every morning.

Papa talked to me a lot about his wife, and how it was when they were first married. He didn't talk so much about their last years, it was mostly about when they was young. He said he knowed it was hard on her when he was running from the law. Said he tried to keep as good a home as he could for her.

Seemed like there was a few things that stayed on his mind, things he told about over and over. One of them was the first home they had there in Groveton. He said she was always laughing, and they was awful happy. He'd tell me how he fixed it up before she got down there, and how she was so happy she cried when she saw it.

Another thing he talked about was the boy he called Little John. That was their second child—the first one was named Horace. Papa would say, "Little John didn't thrive." Said he just got weaker and weaker, and nothing they done for him done any good. He died when he was just a tiny baby. Papa said his wife took it awful hard. Said it hurt him to see her crying all the time. I felt sorry for him. He'd get tears in his eyes when he talked about it. He said they lost a lot of babies while he was running from the law.

They only had Horace left. And then they finally lost him, too. I think he must a been seven or eight years old. That was another thing Papa used to tell me, over and over. He said the law got after him and he had to run. His wife and Horace went to her sister's, and Horace got real sick. Papa said he didn't get there till just before the boy died.

I reckon it must a been really hard to lose him, him being the only one they had left. But what seemed to keep bothering Papa, even all them years later, was that he couldn't understand the way his wife acted when Horace died.

He said the boy was sick with a bad cold when the law got after Papa and he had to leave. The next thing he heard was that his wife and Horace was at her sister Martha's house and Horace had pneumonia. He said he went as fast as he could. And when

[138]

he got there his wife didn't pay no attention to him at all, didn't hardly know he was there. He said she was setting by the boy's bed, wiping his face with wet rags. Said she wasn't crying or anything, and she wasn't talking, she was just wiping the boy's face. Said she kept on wiping his face even after he was dead. Said after he died and they finally got her to stop wiping his face she still didn't cry. She never cried over him at the funeral, even.

Papa said, "It seemed so strange. When we's first married she cried over every little thing. And when Little John died it looked like she'd never stop crying."

Papa's memory started getting bad. Sometimes, I'd be setting there in the living room sewing, or patching or something, and he'd come in there and stand with his back up to the heater and warm himself, and he'd say, "I reckon I'm just gonna have to stay all night with y'all. Looks like I can't catch a ride home."

I'd say, "Well, Papa, we'll be proud to have you stay the night."

Then Fred and Alvin would come in from work, and he'd tell them the same thing. He'd say, "Reckon you can put up with me tonight? I just can't catch a ride home."

I come in from the garden one evening and found him having a fuss with Fred and Alvin. They was trying to help him back to his bedroom. We had a radio in the living room then, and they said Papa was setting there asleep in his chair, snoring, and they couldn't hear the radio, so they was trying to get him to go to bed.

When I got to the door, there was Papa, standing there, leaning on his cane, telling them, "You two leave me alone or I'm gonna take the razor strap to you!"

I had always been able to manage him. I always spoke to him like I meant it—I never let him bluff me. So I walked in there and asked him what was the matter. He said, "They're trying to make me go to bed, and I've only just had my breakfast."

I got in front of him and said, "Come on, Papa. It's after supper, and it's getting dark. You need to go to bed."

He waved that cane and said, "I'll hit you, too. Just see if I won't."

I stood there. I said, "All right, Papa, hit me." And I looked him straight in the eye. He looked at me for a few seconds and then begin to laugh. Then he went along to bed.

He fell off the porch one day and broke some ribs and Fred had to carry him to the hospital. When Fred got ready to come home he told the head nurse, "He might get a little unruly. Do you think you can handle him?"

She said, "Don't worry. That's what we're trained for. We can handle him."

We didn't have no phone then, but Fred give the nurse the number of the store in Nogalus Prairie and told her, "Just in case . . . . You better take this. They'll come and tell me if you need me."

Well, Fred hadn't got home good till that man from the store was here. He said the nurses wanted somebody to come to the hospital, they was having trouble with Papa.

Fred said, "Effie, you can do more with him than I can. You take one of the children and go." So Claud and me went down there.

Some of the nurses was standing in the hall outside Papa's door. They's afraid to go in the room. They said he'd got mad when they tried to help him to the bathroom.

And there was Papa, setting on the edge of the bed, looking like a thundercloud. He had a footstool in his hand, and he was threatening to use it on anybody that got close.

I went in and said, "Papa, what's the matter?"

He said, "I've got to go to the *toilet*! And them fool women are trying to make me take a *bath*!"

I said, "Well, Claud's here. He'll help you find the toilet."

Claud did. And Papa was all right.

He didn't stay in the hospital very long.

Even after Papa was sick, and had to stay in bed most of the time, he still wanted to help with the children. Especially Freddy.

Papa had always paid a lot of attention to Freddy. And when he'd be laying there in bed he'd remember Freddy and he'd call to him: "Freddy! Oh. . . . Freddy! Come here. Papa wants to talk to you."

[140]

Maybe I'd have Freddy in a chair in the living room. He'd hear Papa, and he'd manage to get up on his feet and make his way back to Papa by holding onto the wall down the hall. And Papa would pet him, and talk to him.

Before Papa died, it got to where I had to feed him. He never did give me no trouble. Sometimes he'd think I was his wife. He'd call me Liddie. I'd answer him, just like I was her.

Bibliography

Books and Pamphlets

Aldrich, Armistead Albert. *The History of Houston County.* San Antonio: Naylor, 1943. (Stephen E. Kennedy listed as prominent citizen.)

Allen, Ruth A. *East Texas Lumber Workers.* Austin: University of Texas Press, 1961.

Boatright, Mody C., ed. *The Golden Log.* Dallas: Southern Methodist University Press, 1962.

Boles, Flora G. *A History of Trinity County.* Groveton, Tex.: Groveton Independent School District, 1966. (The lumber industry and way of life in East Texas, late 1800s and early 1900s.)

Bush, Ava. "Ashes—Aid to Man's Advancement." Paper read at convention of Society for Economic Botany, University of Miami, Coral Gables, Florida, May, 1977. (Process for making lye soap.)

Crocket, George Louis. *Two Centuries in East Texas.* Dallas: Southwest Press, 1932.

Day, James M. *Texas Post Office Papers.* Austin: Texas Library and Historical Commission, 1966. (History and organization of early post offices.)

Dobie, J. Frank. *Tales of Old Time Texas.* New York: Little, Brown, 1955.

————. *The Flavor of Texas.* Austin: Jenkins, 1975.

Eagleton, Davis Foute. *Writers and Writings of Texas.* New York: Broadway, 1913. (The establishment of public schools and universities in Texas.)

Haltom, R. W. *History and Description of Angelina County, Texas.* Facsimile. Austin: Pemberton Press, 1969. (Detailed discussion of schools, people, way of life in late 1800s.)

Hogan, William Ranson. *The Texas Republic: A Social and Economic History*. Norman: University of Oklahoma Press, 1946. Facsimile. Austin: University of Texas Press, 1969. (Amount of land received by people migrating to Texas in 1836–37, graphic description of way of life.)

Holbrook, Stewart H. *The Story of American Railroads*. New York: Crown, 1947.

Loetzer, C. E. *Loetzer's Handbook of Practical Rules and Tables for Machinists and Engineers*. Sayre, Pa., 1906. Forestry Museum collection, Lufkin, Texas. (Ways of determining horsepower of steam engines.)

Madden, J. W. "The Madden and Edens Massacre." Typed manuscript in Crockett Public Library, Crockett, Texas (Early settlers in north Houston County, their land acquisition, etc.)

Mullins, Marion Day. *Texas Citizenship Lists and Other Early Records of Republic of Texas*. Washington, D.C.: National Genealogical Society, 1962.

Owens, William A. *This Stubborn Soil*. New York: Charles Scribner's Sons, 1966.

Pennybacker, Anna J. Hardwicke. *A History of Texas*. Austin: published by the author, 1907.

Peery, William, ed. *Twenty-one Texas Short Stories*. Austin: University of Texas Press, 1954.

Ramos, Ralph. *Rocking Texas Cradle*. Beaumont: Enterprise Company, 1974.

Rankin, Melinda, *Texas in 1850*. Boston: Damrell and Moore, 1850. Facsimile. Waco: Texian Press, 1966.

Smithwick, Noah. *The Evolution of a State*. Austin: Gammel Book Company, 1900. Reprint. Austin: Steck-Vaughn, 1935. Facsimile. Austin: Steck-Vaughn, 1968. (Good account of life, law and order, in early and middle 1800s in Texas.)

Stein, Ralph. *The American Automobile*. New York: Random House, n.d. (White Steamer automobiles.)

Stiff, Colonel Edward. *Texas Emigrant*. Cincinnati: George Conclin, 1840. Reprint. Waco: Texian Press, 1968. (Another good book on way of life in East Texas in early 1800s.)

Tinkle, Lon. *13 Days to Glory*. New York: McGraw-Hill, 1958 (Land grants.)

Tolbert, Frank X. *An Informal History of Texas*. New York: Harper, 1961. (Breakdown of law and order following the Civil War.)

Vigness, David M. *The Revolutionary Decades: The Saga of Texas*